Holland's Guide
to Psychoanalytic Psychology
and Literature-and-Psychology

Holland's Guide to Psychoanalytic Psychology and Literature-and-Psychology

Norman N. Holland

New York   Oxford
OXFORD UNIVERSITY PRESS
1990

Oxford University Press

Oxford   New York   Toronto
Delhi   Bombay   Calcutta   Madras   Karachi
Petaling Jaya   Singapore   Hong Kong   Tokyo
Nairobi   Dar es Salaam   Cape Town
Melbourne   Auckland

and associated companies in
Berlin   Ibadan

Published by Oxford University Press, Inc.,
200 Madison Avenue, New York, New York 10016

Oxford is a registered trademark of Oxford University Press

Library of Congress Cataloging-in-Publication Data
Holland, Norman Norwood, 1927–
Holland's guide to psychoanalytic psychology
and literature-and-psychology /
Norman N. Holland.
p.   cm.   Includes bibliographical references.
ISBN 0-19-506279-5.
—ISBN 0-19-506280-9 (pbk.)
1. Psychoanalysis—Outlines, syllabi, etc.
2. Psychoanalysis and literture—Outlines, syllabi, etc.
I. Title.   BF173.H718   1990 150.19'5'0202—dc20
89-38898   CIP

9 8 7 6 5 4 3 2 1

Printed in the United States of America
on acid-free paper

150.195
H736h
1990

Acknowledgments

I AM GRATEFUL to many colleagues, friends, and students for their help in writing and trying out this *Guide*. Michel Grimaud and Paul Kugler were kind enough to write special sections on Jungian criticism and cognitive poetics respectively. William McPheron artfully crafted the original version of the chapter on research aids. Ellie Ragland-Sullivan gave me invaluable assistance and reassurance with the Lacan sections, as did Caryl Flinn with my remarks on film criticism. Bernard Paris shared his knowledge of "third force" materials and has ably directed the Florida Institute while we were trying out this *Guide*. Terry Brown and Barrie Ruth Straus both gave me expert help with the more intricate parts of feminist psychoanalytic criticism. Claire Kahane has directed the Buffalo Center while I was working on this *Guide,* and she too has counseled me on feminist criticism. David Willbern has directed the Buffalo Center, and served as symposiarch, bibliographer, and punster at various occasions where I tried out these ideas. Sam Kimball, Brenda Marshall, and Craig Saper helped as research assistants, finding materials for one who is always losing them and proofreading for one impatient of detail. Laura Keyes supplied more proofreading and her whimsical sense of error and ego. Murray Schwartz has graciously shared, over many years, his encyclopedic knowledge of the psychoanalytic literature. Norman Kiell gave me immensely helpful counsel on the project as a whole. Without their contributions this *Guide* would be much less useful than I hope it is.

Stuart Krichevsky of Sterling Lord Literistic took care of the negotiating, and William Sisler proved an editor of taste and vision. I am grateful, finally, to Dragonfly Software for their *Nota Bene,* which enabled me to produce "camera-ready copy" and to have a momentary sense of what Caxton and William Morris must have felt.

Many other colleagues and students, too many to name here, have made suggestions and have contributed much. I am mindful and appreciative of them all. I do, however, want to memorialize once again my respectful indebtedness to my mentors in psychoanalysis who led me past the magnolia tree at the Boston Psychoanalytic Institute: most memorably, Ives Hendrick, Peter Knapp, Joseph Michaels, Paul Myerson, Harry Rand, and especially Elizabeth Zetzel. Prior to them all, of course, was G. Henry Katz in Philadelphia. And Jane.

I must apologize for the many references to my own prior work. Indeed if you look at the final list of references you will find more entries for me than for Freud. I do not mean to imply that I am more important. It's simply that I have often expressed in writing the ideas that inform this *Guide.* It seemed only sensible in this, as in other matters, to guide you to the primary source.

Gainesville, Florida   *Norman N. Holland*
September 1989

Contents

Holland's Guide
to Psychoanalytic Psychology
and Literature-and-Psychology

1

A Guide to the Guide

I HAVE DESIGNED this *Guide* to provide you, my reader, with a program of reading in what we in the game call, "lit-and-psych" or, slightly more formally, literature-and-psychology. That is shorthand for using psychology, particularly psychoanalytic psychology, to answer questions about literature and the arts. Why do people write and read literature? What do they get out of it? Why does this writer write in this particular style? Why does that character act that way?

I imagine you as someone who simply would like to be able to answer questions like these. Or you would like to talk and think intelligently about the various topics listed in the upcoming outline. Or you may be someone who would like to be able to use psychoanalytic concepts in other, nonpsychological work: literature, history, philosophy, or "theory." You may, then, be looking for a kind of "general education" in psychoanalysis.

Alternatively, you might be someone working more formally in one of the university programs specifically in literature-and-psychology or more generally "theory" or even, now, "psychoanalytic studies." I have worked with such programs at the Institute for Psychological Study of the Arts at the University of Florida and the Center for Psychological Study of the Arts at the State University of New York at Buffalo. Both these programs pose examinations in psychoanalytic psychology. The exams simply ask the student to be literate in psychoanalysis. The most prosaic use for this *Guide*, then, would be to study for such examinations. Chapters 2 and 3, the Topical Outlines, list topics. An examinee might be asked to define, describe, explain, or criticize these topics, drawing on recent as well as early psychoanalytic thinking where they differ. More generally, the ability to handle these topics competently provides a useful basis for dissertations, papers for presentation or publication, but also for larger speculations and the reading of psychoanalytic comments on literature, society, or human nature. You could also use this *Guide* as a self-test: Do I understand this topic? Have I read these authors?

At the same time, I have to admit up front that this effort is futile. Psychoanalysis is the science of human subjectivity. It offers insights into the mind's ways of thinking, dreaming, imagining, wanting, and especially the mind's ways of hiding from itself. Ultimately, each of us has to find those ways out in our own minds since we do not have access to the minds of others. In other words, the laboratory for this science is one's own mind. Without some, so to speak, hands-on experience of psychoanalytic insight into the mind's ways, psychoanalysis becomes dry and abstract. It will seem arbitrary and made-up.

A "reading knowledge" of psychoanalysis, then, is not enough. One needs some experience of unconscious processes. You can get it by undergoing dynamic psychotherapy, psychoanalysis, or even just some of the new modes of teaching that try to give students insight into their own processes. However you get it, you must get it if you are to do serious work in lit-and-psych.

Reading is not enough, yet reading is also necessary alongside that actual experience. To help you with the reading part of your quest is my purpose in this *Guide*. It is a highly structured and focused *Guide*. I believe that simply handing you a bibliography—a list of readings—would not really help in this project because the list would have to be so large. The texts would have to come from all the many stages and perspectives in psychoanalytic thought. A bad effect of the book list approach is to rob psychoanalytic writings of their clinical, social, or historical setting. Treating psychoanalysis just as texts makes it a merely philosophical or literary idea, often just the latest or most fashionable version of psychoanalysis.

Real psychoanalysis stands or falls on a cumulated base of clinical experience. If we ignore that base, we turn psychoanalysis into language games or airy speculation. It is essential to have some clinical experience of psychoanalysis and to supplement that experience with a sense of the historical practice of psychoanalysis. Moreover, in my experience, the more you study psychoanalysis per se, especially clinical psychoanalysis, the better psychoanalytic criticism you will write. It is a mistake to read only psychoanalytic literary criticism and then try to practice it.

For these reasons, I think someone setting out to "read lit-and-psych" needs more than just a list of readings. Hence, although this *Guide* ends with that, a list of readings, the body of the *Guide* provides an intellectual road map. The list rests upon an idea of the clinical, historical, and intellectual development of psychoanalysis.

For the same reasons, you should not expect this list to include all the important books in psychoanalysis. You should not expect to find here everything interesting or worthwhile in lit-and-psych or psychoanalytic psychology. Nor is this a bibliography of everything

psychoanalytic in today's literary, filmic, "cultural," and philosophical studies. You should not expect it to include all the books based
on a nodding acquaintance with psychoanalysis that have appeared
in recent years as literary critics and philosophers have faddishly
taken up psychoanalysis.

This is a tendentious list, one with a purpose. This is a list
designed to give you whatever knowledge reading can of how to
apply clinical psychoanalysisis to literature and the other arts. It is
moreover a list with a lot of opinions behind it. I make no claim that
this is an "objective" survey of psychoanalysis or psychoanalytic
criticism in the usual sense of the word. I believe the essence of psychoanalysis's discoveries is that the self, consciously and unconsciously, styles everything—*everything*—we do from making love to
doing science. Hence there is no such thing as an "objective" (or, in
the philosophers' phrase, "God's eye") view of anything.

Let me put that the other way round. When we try to be
"objective," the best we can do is play by certain rules designed to
minimize personal vagary. Thus we have rules by which we do history or science or bibliographies or literary criticism or psychology
or psychoanalysis. But each of us necessarily follows and enacts and
understands those rules within a certain personal style. Today's cognitive science teaches us that we perceive even tables and chairs
within a personal style, to say nothing of something as controversial
as psychoanalysis. Hence this book is not an "objective" guide to
literature-and-psychology or psychoanalytic psychology. If you
would like to know my partialities now, I describe them in Chapter 5
(pp. 59-75).

Nevertheless, despite my belief that it is impossible, I will do
my best to "tell you the truth." That is, I will try to tell you as
honestly and fully as I can my thoughts about literature-and-

psychology (as in the following brief historical sketch of psycho-analysis).

Psychoanalysis came into being—entered its first phase—near the end of the nineteenth century, when Freud began his ambitious effort to found a psychology that would be a branch of science rather than philosophy. At the same time, academic psychology was also changing from a branch of philosophy to an experimental science. (William James was probably the last person to be simultaneously a psychologist and a philosopher.) At that time, however, and to a large extent even today, these two branches of psychology have not had much to say to each other, although I believe they will in the near future. The question, Is psychoanalysis scientific?, remains a lively issue for all involved.

After this scientific origin, I think of psychoanalysis as having evolved in three chronological phases: a psychology of the uncon-scious (1897-1923), ego psychology (1923-), and a psychology of the self (c. 1950-). The later phases do not replace the earlier ones. Rather, each phase builds on and includes what preceded it, enlarg-ing the field of human behavior psychoanalysis attempts to explain.

One can define these three phases by the polarity psycho-analytic thinkers used to explain events. First, it was conscious as opposed to unconscious. Then, ego vis-à-vis nonego. Today, it is self and not-self. More whimsically, you could contrast these three phases by the parts of speech they would make the word *unconscious* into. In the first phase, it was an adjective but also a noun, referring to a thing, a system, or even a place—a sort of bin—in the brain. In the second phase, when Freud announced that "unconscious" was only descriptive, the word became an adjective and only an adjective, as in "unconscious ego." Now, one major theorist (Schafer) has ingeniously suggested that the word has become an adverb—we

should think in terms of a whole person doing this or that unconsciously.

First-phase, "classical" psychoanalysis explained events as conscious or unconscious or as passing from one state to the other.
Within this large framework, Freud developed certain key ideas
about the working and structure of the mind. The other big insight
of the first phase was an understanding of child development as
having specific stages, residues of which persist into adult life. During this first phase, psychoanalysis primarily addressed pathological
or unusual behavior: neurosis, dreams, symptoms, jokes, or artistic
creativity.

The first stage grew directly from Freud's most basic discovery.
I think it is so fundamental to understanding psychoanalysis that I
shall highlight it:

> *If a patient free associates in connection with a symptom, that
> is, says whatever comes to mind without holding anything back,
> sooner or later that patient will enunciate (over strongly felt
> resistance) a repressed thought or feeling that the symptom
> expresses.*

Similarly, if a patient free associates to a dream, the patient will
become aware (against resistance) of a previously unconscious wish.
Freud found the same thing with jokes and with lapses of memory,
forgettings, and slips of the tongue or pen or limbs (called *parapraxes*). Further, free association would work not only for neurotic
patients, but for the parapraxes and jokes and dreams of ordinary
people also (as Freud found in his lifelong self-analysis).

In all these odd, marginal behaviors, free association reveals a
resisted latent or unconscious content underneath a tolerated
manifest or conscious behavior. As Freud realized this manifest-

latent pattern occurred in so many different spheres of mental activity, he concluded that he was doing more than explaining some oddments of human behavior. He had arrived at something fundamental to human nature itself, a general principle of psychological explanation, the struggle between "the" conscious and "the" unconscious.

Gradually, it became clear that this polarity applied not only to odd or marginal behaviors, but to every aspect of daily life from the most abstruse intellectual thought to the most primitive urges of rage or lust. It applied to every kind of person from the wisest to the maddest. In this "classical" phase, Freud thought of conscious and unconscious as opposed forces, as systems or even places. He and his first followers explained overt behaviors and mental events as expressions or repressions of unconscious material occurring when psychic energy shifted from one state to the other.

In the other major discovery of the first phase, psychoanalysts came to understand child development as having specific stages leading to a style or *character* in adult life. In particular, character developed from the child's resolution of its oedipus complex (between, say, ages three and five). At that time, the child is finding and making its place in a world divided into genders, male and female, and generations, parent and child. First-phase psychoanalysts discovered that your style of adult relatedness to other people grew out of the way you coped with your love and hate toward mother and father as you made your way into that gendered and generationed world. Even earlier, the child developed "character," a style of being, from the way it learned to adapt internally to adult concerns about the management of the child's body in feeding, seeing, defecating, urinating, masturbating, or walking. Second and third stage psychoanalysts found that these earlier *oral*, *anal*, and *phallic* stages, because they were earlier, played an even more decisive role in character than the oedipal.

Within this first-phase framework, Freud developed ideas of great generality about the working and structure of the mind. These explanations in terms of a childhood or a repressed unconscious struggling against an adult conscious mind are powerful. Good work was done and good work is still being done using them.

Freud himself, however, found after a quarter-century that clinical experience required him to revise his first theories. In this second phase of his thought, Freud complicated the simple division of the mind into conscious and unconscious by mapping it onto the "structural" hypothesis. In this second phase the mind's workings consisted not of a simple polarity, but of the interaction of id, super-ego, reality, and repetition compulsion under the governance of a presiding ego. *Id*, one would define today as the psychic representation of biological drives. The *superego*, we can think of as the incorporated commands of one's parents, both to do and not to do, violation of which leads to guilt or depression. The *repetition compulsion* means the human tendency to try old solutions even on new problems. The *ego* is the synthesizer and executive that chooses strategies and tactics that best balance these competing needs. *Conscious* and *unconscious* became adjectives applied to the new structures. To most theorists, the id was all unconscious, but there was conscious ego and unconscious, conscious superego and unconscious.

Freud and his colleagues of the 1930s expanded their account of defense mechanisms from repression alone, making the conscious unconscious. The defenses now included many strategies, such as reversing anger into kindness, projecting one's own impulses onto others, or isolating one thought or feeling from another. Freud himself revised the theory of the instincts to include aggressive as well as sexual drives. Heinz Hartmann posited autonomous ego functions that linked psychoanalysis to such topics in orthodox psychology as perception, learning, memory, or motility. This second phase psychoanalysis is usually called *ego psychology*. It spread all over the world as the early psychoanalysts of Germany and Austria and Hungary fled the Third Reich.

The third phase took place largely after Freud's death in 1939. Psychoanalytic psychology went beyond the ego to address the self in the largest sense and, finally, all of human behavior. In the first phase, the basic explanation was "the" unconscious as against "the" conscious. In the second, it was ego versus non-ego. In the third, it became self and non-self. As early as 1930, in the first chapter of *Civilization and Its Discontents*, Freud began this third phase: "Originally the ego includes everything; later it separates off an external world from itself." He had recognized that at least during the beginning of an individual's life span, the wholly *intra*psychic model he had used in the first two phases had to give way to an *inter*psychic model, one that included both the individual mind and its surround.

It remained for others to develop this third phase, however. As Freud and his circle in Vienna were making these large changes in psychoanalytic theory, Nazi persecutions forced their emigration and spread second- and third-phase psychoanalysis all over the world, except in the German-occupied countries. In the process, psychoanalysis acquired different styles in different nations. Indeed, some of these styles are inconsistent with one another, so that psychoanalysis often seems today no longer a unified discipline. It now reflects the diversity of the various intellectual cultures that have made psychoanalysis their own.

In the United States, from the 1950s through the 1970s, Erik Erikson and his followers directed psychoanalysis toward the mutual interaction of personal identity with cultural, political, and anthropological factors in the environment. Increasingly, psychoanalysts began to consider the interaction ("mutuality") between a society that sustained and shaped the individual and an individual who shaped and sustained—and sometimes led—the society. Erikson's theories had great influence on biographical, historical, religious, and political writing, but less on literature and philosophy. It was another theory of identity, Heinz Lichtenstein's, that (at least in my view) bore fruit in literary studies.

In England, a cadre of outstanding psychoanalysts (among them, Melanie Klein, Ronald Fairbairn, and D. W. Winnicott) in the 1940s and 1950s challenged or changed Freud's biological "instinct theory." These "object relations" theorists substituted an account of child development based on interpersonal encounters between the child and its significant others.   Freud had posited as the roots of human motivation innate sexual and aggressive drives and an even deeper, but also biological, "Nirvana principle" (a drive toward minimal excitation).   By contrast, the British "middle school" theorized an instinctual need to relate to other people.   It was in those relationships, rather than from bodily drives, that the child learned different styles of loving and hating.   Concentration on these pre-oedipal experiences led to a more comprehensive account of the themes in the child's development that persisted in the adult's style. The oedipus complex is only one among several critical events. Indeed the child's first-year relation to the mother quite overshadows what Freud had thought dominant, the relation to the father in the third year and after.   Hence the British school is sometimes at odds with conservative analysts, particularly in America.

In France, Jacques Lacan (1901-1981) and those who followed him (starting about 1965) turned toward understanding conscious and unconscious experiences as an entry into a linguistic culture.

Lacan deliberately chose an arcane, metaphorical way to write, describing concerns of the third phase of psychoanalysis (object relations or personal style) in the language of the first phase (phallus, castration). This obscurity has necessitated a great many explications of his thought. Nevertheless, because of his emphasis on language, many literary critics of a philosophical turn have adopted Lacan with enthusiasm, applying his principles to cultural as well as literary theory. Because Lacan treated conscious and unconscious as at odds, the self, as Lacan portrayed it, is split, divided, or alienated. Hence his ideas conflict with concepts like the "identity" of Erikson or Lichtenstein and even the ego as described in second-phase psychoanalysis.

More recently, in the United States, Heinz Kohut has developed a "self-psychology" based on the development of the individual's capacity for realistic self-love alongside the traditional psychoanalytic account of child development through drives or libidinal stages. Both in Kohut's and Otto Kernberg's alternative version, these new theories of the "borderline personality" have become highly influential among American therapists. At the same time, however, they tend to conflict with the traditional account of child development and therapy embodied in second-phase psychoanalysis. There have been vigorous debates in the American psychoanalytic scene.

Margaret Mead cannily pointed out that Freud's theories about women were those of a six-year-old boy. In reaction to this, the weakest part of first- and second-phase psychoanalysis, the 1970s and 1980s have seen emerge a lively feminist critique and revision of psychoanalysis. It cuts across national boundaries although it derives particularly from Lacan and British object-relations theory.

The most recent development in psychoanalysis has taken place primarily in the United States, United Kingdom, West Germany, and Israel. Some psychoanalytic thinkers are trying to connect the psychoanalytic model of the human being with "cognitive science," that is, with cognitive psychology (the principles developed from experiments in perception, cognition, and memory); with the simulation of intelligence on computers; and with neuroscientific research into the functioning of the brain. This merger represents a return to the scientific origins of psychoanalysis, as against the recent claim that psychoanalysis is merely a system for interpreting language. It also seems to me an immensely promising avenue.

Like other sciences, psychoanalysis has its internal conflicts. Sometimes these are matters of fashion. Sometimes they reach to fundamental questions. Like other sciences, psychoanalysis has evolved through stages and continues to evolve. The most recent thinking in psychoanalysis incorporates and generalizes some of Freud's first work in the same way that Einstein's relativity theory incorporates and generalizes Newton's laws of motion. Nevertheless, one cannot learn psychoanalysis as one might learn physics or biology, by studying the "state of the art," that is, the way the science is today. Perhaps what we mean by a "mature" science is just that, one that can be studied ahistorically. In any case, I do not think it is a good idea in the 1980s to study psychoanalysis by reading only the contemporary versions, and certainly not just one of them. Both the theory and the data of psychoanalysis are embedded in a human context.

To be sure, Freud thought of himself, and subsequent psychoanalysts think of themselves, as working within a cumulative science. In this model, psychoanalytic principles cumulate as they are confirmed by clinical experience or, more rarely, by experiment. Nevertheless clinical data are notoriously subject to the theoretical and other preconceptions of the clinician. Even experimental results reflect the biases of the experimenter. We do well to keep in mind what those biases or preconceptions are for any given piece of psychoanalytic writing. They are necessarily rooted in the history of psychoanalysis, especially its conflicts.

Because psychoanalysis has traditionally regarded itself as a science, one should read psychoanalytic literature keeping that claim in mind. One should also be mindful of the view widely held today that psychoanalysis is not a science, but a *hermeneutic*, a system for interpreting texts—language. In addition to its scientific and hermeneutic claims, psychoanalysis shares certain metapsychological points of view. By *metapsychology*, Freud meant the types of statement required in a full psychoanalytic account of an event. One should read any psychoanalytic paper with those five points of view in mind. (They appear in the Topical Outline below.)

The Topical Outline (Chapter 2) provides a list and organization of the above themes in Chapter 1. In using this *Guide*, you will find it helpful, I think, to read Chapter 2 in the light of this "Guide to the *Guide*," and the "Guide" against Chapter 2. Chapter 3, the Topical Outline Keyed, then adds to that first list citations for the appropriate books and articles in the list of references that is Chapter 7. Whenever possible, I have listed readings in the Topical Outline Keyed so as to lead one deeper and deeper into a given topic. First on the list will be summarizing statements, introductions, or guides to the idea. Later items will give more complex, detailed, or primary accounts. You should be able to read, therefore, any topic in the Outline at whatever level of complexity seems right to you. You should, however, be aware that, given the literary aims of this *Guide*, I have completely omitted one major topic: therapy and therapeutic techniques. Also, although they are fascinating, I have not tried to survey the growing number of biographical studies of such major psychoanalytic figures as Freud, Jung, Ernest Jones, Melanie Klein, Karen Horney, and others.

Chapter 4 applies the intellectual map to literature-and-psychoanalysis (or, more precisely, literature-and-psychology and not just literature but occasionally other arts as well). Here again, the readings listed in the outline refer to items in the references in the last chapter of this *Guide*. As you encounter items in that list of readings, keep in mind what led you to them them in Chapters 2, 3, 4, and 5. The prose describing them and their position in the various outlines constitute annotations of what would otherwise be an alphabetized reading list devoid of signposts. Again, as with Chapters 1 and 2, look back and forth from chapter to chapter.

I have resisted the temptation to include any and all good things to read in psychoanalysis in Chapter 7. My aim in this *Guide* is to provide a relatively small, focused, manageable reading list. There are enough long psychoanalytic booklists already. If you want more, Chapter 6, Research Aids, gives an account of the various bibliographies, dictionaries, concordances, and indexes that one could use to expand the bibliography of Chapter 7 or to research a given psychoanalytic topic or author in depth.

Chapter 5 is an epilogue in which I express my opinions more explicitly than in the rest of this idiosyncratic *Guide*. It also lists some light reading and poses a heavy question, Where are psychoanalysis and literature-and-psychology going from here? At the moment, at least, to Chapter 2.

2

A Topical Outline

THE OUTLINE THAT follows is designed to give you an organiz-
ing set of files, so to speak, within which to put your reading and
knowledge of psychoanalysis: three phases and various issues and
schools within those phases. Incidentally, notice that I have begun
numbering the outline with 0. Please forgive this eccentricity. I took
my cue from computer numbering (0, 1, 2), so as to avoid the confu-
sion of "2. First phase . . . 3. Second phase . . . ".

As you read this outline, keep in mind the basic objective of the
Guide. It is to organize readings so that you can think and talk intelligently about the various topics listed. This chapter gives the topics.
I have used an outline form that I hope will enable you to carry them
in your head as you read further. Chapter 3 gives the same topics
keyed to readings. Chapter 4 gives the same topics as they relate to
literature-and-psychology.

A Topical Outline

0.   Overview of psychoanalysis since its origins.

   a.   3 historical phases of psychoanalysis:

      1890-1923   Cs and Ucs; id-psychology
      1923-   Ego and non-ego; ego-psychology
      ca. 1950-   Self and non-self; psychology of self and
                   other

   b.   5 metapsychological points of view:

      dynamic
      economic
      genetic/developmental
      topographic (first phase); then
      structural (second phase)
         id
         ego
         superego
      adaptive
      a sixth: personal

   c.   Psychoanalysis as science:

      a hermeneutic
      holistic method
      and linguistics
      and experimentation

1. First-phase psychoanalysis (Freud).

    a. Key terms:

        unconscious (descriptive, systemic, dynamic, repressed,
          infantile), preconscious, conscious
        instinctual drives
        representation
        wish
        pleasure-unpleasure principle
        reality principle
        primary and secondary processes
        symbol

    b. Stages of child development:

        oral (see 3-b)
        anal
        urethral
        phallic
        oedipal
        the classical paradigm of male and female development

2. Second-phase psychoanalysis (ego-psychology).

    a. Freud's reasons for the shift:

        repetitions and the compulsion to repeat

    b. Structural hypothesis: id, ego, superego.

    c. Principle of multiple function (four-pole model):

ego facing id, superego, reality, compulsion to repeat
inward and outward adaptation

d. Autonomous ego functions: primary; secondary.

e. Defense mechanisms (acronym PRUDIST):

projection
repression, regression, reversal, reaction-formation
undoing
denial (disavowal), doing and undoing
incorporation, introjection, identification; identification
    with the aggressor; isolation; intellectualization
suppression; sublimation; sexualizing
turning against the self

f. Aggressive/death instinct (Eros and Thanatos).

3. Third-phase psychoanalysis.

a. Psychosocial theory:

epigenetic ground plan
life stages (eight?)
psychosocial identity

b. Object-relations theory, as contrasted to instinctual-
biological:

the first year of life
five "oral tasks":
    tolerance of delay
    tolerance of ambivalence

      self-object differentiation
      separation of inside and outside
      symbolization
   transitional object
   potential space
   relation to cognitive skills

c.   Identity theory:

   primary identity
   identity principle
   identity theme
   DEFT
   relation to perception, object relations, reading—ARC
   "Delphi" teaching

d.   Third force psychology:

   real self
   hierarchy of basic needs
   self-actualization vs. self-alienation
   world openness vs. embeddedness
   transparency, congruence, spontaneity
   authoritarian vs. humanistic conscience
   interpersonal and intrapsychic strategies of defense
   relation to Freudian theory

e.   "French Freud":

   the mirror stage
   the signifier-signified relation and its *glissement*
   desire and demand
   the Real, the Imaginary, the Symbolic

the penis/phallus
nom du père

f.   Narcissism theory:

Kohut's version
Kernberg's version

the "self-object" (Kohut) or self-object-affect cluster
   (Kernberg)
narcissism vs. object-libido (Kohut)
dual development (Kohut)
grandiose self (Kohut)
idealized parent-imago
sense of cohesion of self

g.   Feminist psychoanalysis:

patriarchal society
differential parenting
rewriting Freud
Lacanian approaches

h.   Cognitive psychology and psychoanalysis:

Piaget
infant psychology and development
brain architecture and chemistry
synthesis

3

The Topical Outline Keyed

THIS CHAPTER for the *Guide* consists of the same topical outline as Chapter 2 (including my starting with 0). Now, however, it is keyed to readings. That is, the Topical Outline (Chapter 2) provides a list and organization of important topics in psychoanalytic psychology. The Topical Outline Keyed adds to that first list references to the appropriate books and articles in the References that make up Chapter 7. Whenever possible, I have listed readings in the following way: the first items under a given topic are likely to be simple, summarizing statements, secondary (or even tertiary) rather than primary. Later items are more complex and detailed accounts, and the last are the primary sources for the idea. You should, therefore, be able to explore any topic in the Outline at whatever level of complexity you feel you need. Some items you may feel you can skip entirely. You may want to probe others in depth. Look back and forth from the References to this chapter because the place of an item in this Outline constitutes an annotation on it.

In this chapter, I have listed most references simply by author and date (enough to elicit full bibliographic data in the bibliography in Chapter 7). I have abbreviated Freud simply as SF and all references to Freud are keyed to the *Standard Edition* (see the first Freud entry in Chapter 7). That is, a date with a letter added, like 1901b, refers to 1901b in the *Standard Edition*'s Freud bibliography and such other aids as the Freud abstracts, concordance, or German-English paginator. For other authors 1901b would refer to the second 1901 item in the bibliography of Chapter 7. Occasionally, both with Freud and with other authors, I have included short titles or page or chapter references where I believed they would enable you to read the outline more meaningfully.

The Topical Outline Keyed

0. Overview of classical psychoanalysis.

    a. 3 historical phases of psychoanalysis (Holland 1985, 355-63; 1976a, 1986a):

        | 1890-1923 | Cs and Ucs; id-psychology |
        | 1923- | Ego and non-ego; ego-psychology |
        | ca. 1950- | Self and non-self; psychology of self and other |

    b. 5 metapsychological points of view (Holland 1985, 79-82; Rapaport & Gill 1959):

        dynamic
        economic
        genetic/developmental

topographic (first phase); then
structural (second phase) (Arlow & Brenner 1964)
   id
   ego
   superego
adaptive (Rapaport & Gill 1959)
a sixth: personal (Holland 1985, 79-82)

c. Psychoanalysis as science:

a hermeneutic (Meissner 1966, 1971)
holistic method (Diesing 1971)
and linguistics (Schafer 1970, 1976, 1978; Edelson 1972)
and experimentation (Kline 1972; Fisher & Greenberg
   1977)

1. First-phase psychoanalysis.
Look up terms in Laplanche & Pontalis 1968; Moore &
Fine 1967; Rycroft 1968.
General introductions to psychoanalysis that are useful for
this phase: Appignanesi & Zarate 1979; SF 1916-1917; Waelder
1960, 1964; Hendrick 1958; Alexander 1948; Wollheim 1971;
Gilman 1982; Jones 1953-57 (use index).
Readings from Freud: SF 1989; SF 1986.

a. key terms:

unconscious (descriptive, systemic, dynamic, repressed,
   infantile), preconscious, conscious (Strachey 1953-
   1974; SF 1905c, 1915e)
instinctual drives (E. Bibring 1941)
representation (Schimek 1975; Laplanche & Pontalis
   1968, s.v. "Thing-Presentation"; SF 1915e, 201)

wish (SF 1900a, 566-568)
pleasure-unpleasure principle (SF 1911b)
reality principle (SF 1911b)
primary and secondary processes (Noy 1969; SF 1900a,
    ch. VII-E)
symbol (Rycroft 1974, 1979; SF 1915-16, Lect. X; Jones
    1916)

b. stages of child development (Buxbaum 1959; SF 1905d):

    oral (see 3-b)
    anal (Abraham 1921; Jones 1918; SF 1908b)
    urethral (Michaels 1955)
    phallic (Lewin 1933; Reich 1949)
    oedipal (Fenichel 1931)
    the classical paradigm of male and female development
        (Chodorow 1978, ch. 1; Mitchell 1974, Part I)

2. Second-phase psychoanalysis: ego-psychology (Rapaport 1959;
    Fenichel 1945).
        General introductions: Moore & Fine 1967; Waelder 1960,
    1964; Hendrick 1958; Bernstein & Warner 1981; Brenner 1973.

    a. Freud's reasons for the shift (SF 1923b):

        repetitions and the compulsion to repeat (SF 1920g;
            Jones 1953-1957, 3: 268-69, 272; Schur 1972, ch. 12)

    b. Structural hypothesis: id, ego, superego (SF 1933a, XXXI-
        XXXII).

    c. Principle of multiple function (four-pole model):

ego faces id, superego, reality, compulsion to repeat (Waelder 1930)
inward and outward adaptation (Hartmann 1939, 1964)

d.   Autonomous ego functions: primary; secondary (Hartmann 1964)

e.   Defense mechanisms (acronym PRUDIST) (G. Bibring 1961; Schafer 1968; Laughlin 1979):

projection
repression, regression, reversal, reaction-formation
undoing
denial (disavowal), doing and undoing
incorporation, introjection, identification (Meissner 1970-1972); identification with the aggressor; isolation; intellectualization
suppression; sublimation; sexualizing
turning against the self

f.   Aggressive or death instinct: Eros and Thanatos (Laplanche 1976; E. Bibring 1941; SF 1920g).

3.   Third-phase psychoanalysis (Reppen 1985).

a.   Psychosocial theory (Erikson 1963, 1968):

epigenetic ground plan
life stages (eight?)
psychosocial identity

b.   Object-relations theory, as contrasted to instinctual-
biological (Fairbairn 1963; Chodorow 1978, chs. 3, 4, and
7; Guntrip 1969; Eagle 1984; Greenberg & Mitchell
1983; Hughes 1989; Buckley 1986; Kohon 1986):

the first year of life (Spitz 1965; Mahler 1975; Stern
1985)
five "oral tasks" (Holland 1985, chs. 7-8):
tolerance of delay
tolerance of ambivalence
self-object differentiation
separation of inside and outside
symbolization
transitional object (Grolnick & Barkin 1978; Winnicott
1953)
potential space (Grolnick & Barkin 1978; Winnicott
1953, 1966)
relation to cognitive skills (Stern 1971, 1985)

c.   Identity theory (Holland 1985; Lichtenstein 1977):

primary identity (Lichtenstein 1961)
identity principle (Lichtenstein 1963)
identity theme (Holland 1985, Part I)
DEFT (Holland 1985, 1975, 1976b)
relation to perception, object relations, reading—ARC
(Holland 1985, 100-106; 1975, 1976b)
"Delphi" teaching (Holland & Schwartz 1975; Holland
1977, 1978)

d.   Third force psychology (Paris 1986):

real self (Horney 1950; Maslow 1968, 1970)

hierarchy of basic needs (Maslow 1970)
self-actualization (Maslow 1968) vs. self-alienation
(Horney 1950)
world openness vs. embeddedness (Schachtel 1959)
transparency, congruence, spontaneity (Rogers 1961)
authoritarian vs. humanistic conscience (Fromm 1947)
interpersonal and intrapsychic strategies of defense
(Horney 1945, 1950; Laing 1965)
relation to Freudian theory (Horney 1939; Schachtel
1959)

e. "French Freud" (Laplanche & Pontalis 1968; Turkle
1978):
Introductions to and explanations of Lacan (in
order of readability): Benvenuto & Kennedy 1986; Clément 1983; Schneiderman 1983; Muller & Richardson
1982; Ragland-Sullivan 1986; Bär 1974; Felman 1987;
Lemaire 1977

the mirror stage (Lacan 1949)
the signifier-signified relation and its *glissement* (Lacan
1957)
desire and demand (Lacan 1956a)
the Real, the Imaginary, the Symbolic (Laplanche &
Pontalis s.v.; Sheridan 1966):
the penis/phallus (Lacan 1958)
nom du père (Lacan 1958)

f. Narcissism theory (Eagle 1984):

Kohut's version: summaries by Greenberg &
Mitchell 1983; Kohut & Wolf 1978; Ornstein 1974;

Kohut 1971, 1977
   Kernberg's version: Greenberg & Mitchell 1983;
   Kernberg 1975, 1978

Kohut's "self-object" or Kernberg's self-object-affect
cluster (Kernberg 1975)
narcissism vs. object-libido (Kohut 1977)
dual development (Kohut 1977)
grandiose self (Kohut 1971)
idealized parent-imago (Kohut 1971; Kernberg 1978)
sense of cohesion of self (Kohut 1977; Kernberg 1975)

g.   Feminist psychoanalysis (Alpert 1986):

patriarchal society (Mitchell 1974)
differential parenting (Chodorow 1978)
rewriting Freud (Bernheimer & Kahane 1985)
Lacanian approaches (Gallop 1982; Irigaray 1977; Marks
   & de Courtivron 1980; Mitchell & Rose 1982)

h.   Cognitive psychology and psychoanalysis (Grimaud
     1984):

Piaget (Wolff 1960; Beard 1969)
infant psychology and development (Stern 1971, 1985;
   Belsky 1982)
brain architecture and chemistry (Harris 1986; Winson
   1985)
synthesis (Holland 1985; Erdelyi 1985; Palombo 1978;
   Reppen 1981; Peterfreund 1980)

4

Literature-and-Psychology

BY LITERATURE-AND-PSYCHOLOGY, I mean the application of psychology to explore literary problems and behavior. (Occasionally, however, I will refer in this summary to other arts: film, music, or painting.) People sometimes speak of "psychological criticism," which is literary criticism using a formal psychology to analyze the writing or reading or content of literary texts. Either way, however, what defines the field is the explicit use of a formal psychology, and the psychology that literary critics most commonly use is psychoanalytic psychology.

In the largest sense, all criticism is psychological criticism, since all criticism and theory proceed from assumptions about the psychology of the humans who make or experience or are portrayed in literature. When Plato speaks of poetry enfeebling the mind or of poetic creation as a divine madness, when Aristotle writes of catharsis or Coleridge of imagination, they are making psychological statements.

Literature also embodies the psychological assumptions of its makers, and literature is realized through the psychological assumptions of its interpreters. Hence, historical critics will turn to the psychological beliefs of the Renaissance to explicate the plays of Shakespeare or the criticism of Jonson. Twentieth-century critics also use psychological assumptions, even critics who posit an "objective" text—they posit a perception of that text independent of the activities of the perceiver's mind. Some twentieth-century critics leave their psychological assumptions tacit or derive them from common sense or philosophy, not psychology as such. Most twentieth-century critics, however, make their psychological assumptions formal and explicit.

Hence, psychological criticism, properly so called, dates from the first efforts at the end of the nineteenth century to create experimental, clinical, or "scientific" psychologies separate from aesthetic or philosophical statements about the nature of the human. From that time to the present, psychological criticism has drawn primarily on three psychologies: psychoanalytic (Freudian), archetypal (or analytic or Jungian), and cognitive psychology.

Psychologies, however, deal in the first instance not with poems or stories, but persons. Hence, psychological criticism will discuss the author, some member(s) of the author's audience, a character, or "the language" (and that usually means a character or some psychological process represented in the language). It is useful, therefore, when thinking about *literature*-and-psychology to keep in mind what *person* is being discussed. At this point, notice the several divisions of psychoanalytic criticism: three phases of psychoanalysis, three persons in literature—it is useful in thinking about any given piece of psychoanalytic criticism to "situate" it in the appropriate one of the nine categories.

The outline that has served so far necessarily blurs when we turn from psychoanalysis per se to psychoanalysis applied to literature or the arts. Despite the change in emphasis I shall keep the headings that I hope have become familiar by now, but I will be more essayistic here and more inclusive. I will introduce two topics in literature-and-psychology, close to being but not, strictly, "psychoanalytic." That is, I will suggest where Jungian literary criticism touches on Freudian. I will also digress at length on what seems to me one of the most important places for psychology in the current critical scene: reader-response criticism.

Literature-and-Psychology Outline (Headings Only)

0. Overview of psychoanalysis since its origins.

    a. 3 historical phases of psychoanalysis:

1890-1923	Cs and Ucs; id-psychology
1923-	Ego and non-ego; ego-psychology
ca. 1950-	Self and non-self; psychology of self and other

1. First-phase psychoanalysis.

    a. Freud himself
    b. Psychoanalysts besides Freud
    c. Literary critics
    d. Archetypal (Jungian) criticism

2. Second-phase psychoanalysis (ego-psychology).

Freud's reasons for the shift
structural hypothesis: id, ego, superego
principle of multiple function (four-pole model)
autonomous ego functions: primary; secondary
defense mechanisms: projection, repression, undoing, etc.

aggressive/death instinct (Eros and Thanatos).

    a.   Freud himself
    b.   Biography
    c.   Criticism and theory

3.   Third-phase psychoanalysis (b-i and i are new).

    a.   Psychosocial theory
    b.   Object-relations theory, as contrasted to instinctual-biological
    b-   i. Modern Jungian criticism
    c.   Identity theory and "Delphi" teaching
    d.   Third force psychology
    e.   "French Freud"
    f.   Narcissism theory
    g.   Feminist psychoanalysis
    h.   Cognitive psychology
    i.   Reader-response criticism

Despite the expansion of our outline, this remains simply a guide for someone who wants to begin studying literature-and-psychology, a road map rather than a geological survey of the area. There are a number of excellent, longer surveys listed in section 0, "Overview." As in the other sections of this *Guide* I have listed texts (unless otherwise indicated) in order of generality: surveys and summaries first, primary sources last.

I have concentrated on theory and methods rather than practical criticism of particular texts and authors because I think someone starting to read in this field does well to become familiar with the issues involved, the "theory" currently so popular in literary circles. Where there are no theoretical texts I have occasionally resorted to practical criticism demonstrating a certain position. On the whole, though, if you want to look up psychological criticism specifically directed to Shakespeare or Keats or Dickens, you should turn to the aids to research in Chapter 6.

By far the largest body of psychological criticism draws on psychoanalytic psychology, perhaps because from the very beginning Freud was concerned with the exact wording of a patient's free associations, a slip of the tongue, or the telling of a dream or a joke. Hence, psychoanalytic psychology lends itself particularly well to the study of details of poetic language. Also, since the 1960s, psychoanalysis has become more and more a general psychology, as theorists have drawn on anthropology, experiments, neuroscience, and such modern theories as semiotics or information theory. Controversies that looked big in the 1920s, like Freud vs. Jung, now seem small as psychoanalysis has become a psychology of the self.

Literature-and-Psychology Outline Keyed

0. Overview of psychoanalysis since its origins.

   a.   3 historical phases of psychoanalysis:

1890-1923	Cs and Ucs; id-psychology
1923-	Ego and non-ego; ego-psychology
ca. 1950-	Self and non-self; psychology of self and other

Here, in chronological order, are a number of general surveys or commentaries on the application of psychoanalysis or psychology in general to literature (and, sometimes, the other arts): Hoffman 1957; Grimaud 1976; Holland 1976a, 1978a; Skura 1981; Winner

1982; Grimaud 1982; Schwartz & Willbern 1982; Grimaud 1984; Wright 1984; Natoli & Rusch 1984; Holland 1986a.

1.   First-phase psychoanalysis.

    a.   Freud himself

Literature played a key role in Freud's discovery of psychoanalysis. In the letter of October 15, 1897, in which he announced that he had found love of the mother and jealousy of the father in his self-analysis, he went on to identify this complex with the "gripping power" of *Oedipus Rex* and the unconscious forces behind Shakespeare's writing of *Hamlet*, as well as that prince's inability to act. He thus addressed all three of the persons of psychological criticism, although in this first phase he confined his writings largely to author or character.

In "Creative Writers and Day-Dreaming" (1908e), Freud developed a powerful model of the literary process. The writer, stimulated by a present wish, enriches it unconsciously with wishes from childhood and embodies it in a literary form that entices an audience (who in their turn take the text as stimulus and elaborate it with *their* unconscious wishes). Using this model, he wrote studies of Leonardo da Vinci and Dostoevsky and his longest literary analysis, an interpretation of the dreams in Jensen's novella *Gradiva*. He also analyzed a variety of literary characters: Hamlet, Macbeth and Lady Macbeth, Ibsen's Rebecca West, and Falstaff (Holland 1966; Spector 1973; Strachey 1961).

    b.   Psychoanalysts besides Freud

Freud's writings prompted a number of other early psychoanalytic figures to literary criticism. Jens Fischer's 1980 anthology collects many of these first-phase pieces. Typical writings were Ernest Jones's study of *Hamlet* ([1910] 1949), Otto Rank's remarkable analysis of myths (1926), Marie Bonaparte's analysis of Poe (1933), and Phyllis Greenacre's studies of Swift and Carroll (1955). Characteristically, these first-phase psychoanalytic critics used only such early psychoanalytic concepts as "unconscious content," the oedipus complex, and the phallic and anal stages of child development. They treated characters mimetically, as real persons manifesting clinical entities. Typically, such critics also relied heavily on psychoanalytic jargon and Freud's lists of symbols in the 1914 additions to *The Interpretation of Dreams* or the first set of *Introductory Lectures* in 1915-17 (a tactic that resulted in some bizarre criticism and a bad reputation for psychoanalytic studies among conventional literary critics).

c.   Literary critics

Perhaps because it was so novel, this first-phase style, the search for a latent content, set the image of psychoanalytic criticism in literary circles. Also, a number of prominent literary critics of the 1930s, 1940s, and 1950s, began to use this first phase of psychoanalytic theory: William Empson (1935), Edmund Wilson (1929, 1948), Lionel Trilling (1953), Kenneth Burke (1941, 1966), Leslie Fiedler (1960), and others represented in the first edition (1957) of William Phillips's anthology or described in Claudia Morrison's history of this movement (1968). Psychoanalytic criticism extended into film with Wolfenstein and Leites' 1950 study of motifs in American, British, and French movies. In this first phase, psychoanalysis had great influence on writers as well as critics, as surveyed by Hoffman (1945, 1957) or, for drama, Sievers (1955).

Criticism in this first phase style continues, sampled in such anthologies as Crews's (1970) or Kaplan and Kloss's (1973), and some of it remains highly effective precisely because of the simplicity and economy of its theory. Harold Bloom's well-known model of poetic influence (1973), for example, rests on Freud's early version of the oedipus complex. Gallop's account of feminism's relation to psychoanalysis draws on early Freudian models of the family (1982): psychoanalysis is the father, feminism the daughter. (Contrast Gardiner [1976] for whom psychoanalysis is the mother for feminism.) Some excellent psychoanalytic criticism of film is also written in first-phase style (Greenberg 1975; Derwin 1985).

    d.   Archetypal (Jungian) criticism

    Because of this emphasis on symbolism and a relatively few explanatory terms, early psychoanalytic and early archetypal (or Jungian) criticism often resemble each other. Hence, this is a good place to quote a brief description of Jungian theory written for this *Guide* by Paul Kugler:

> Archetypal criticism has been a significant force in criticism since the 1920s. Its theoretical foundation derives from the work of the Swiss psychoanalyst Carl Jung, especially his idea that archetypal structures are the primary factors organizing human personality. For Jung, the personal unconscious consists of memories and images (imagos) collected in the course of an individual life. The collective unconscious, on the other hand, is limited to the imposition of structural laws—archetypes. The personal unconscious is like a lexicon where each of us accumulates an individual vocabulary, but these lexical units acquire value and significance only in so far as they are archetypally structured. If the unconscious activity of the psyche consists in imposing structures (archetypes) upon content (imagos), and if these

structures are fundamentally the same for all personalities, then to understand and interpret a literary text psychologically it is necessary to analyze the unconscious structures underlying the text itself. This is the model used in traditional Jungian criticism.

Jung published the first archetypal analysis of a literary text in 1912 in "Wandlungen und Symbole der Libido," an extensive analysis of the archetypal structures underlying Longfellow's *Hiawatha*. In this analysis, Jung introduced his interpretative method known as *amplification*. Earlier, Freud had demonstrated the importance of free association for understanding the unconscious motivation and meaning of a person's dream. Jung extended this idea not only to the personal associations of the dreamer, but also to intertextual associations within the dreamer's cultural canon, and in some cases, cross-cultural associations as well. By establishing a larger intertextual context for the dream image through philological, iconological, mythological, and historical research, the process of amplification deliteralizes the image, cultivating an attitude that psychologically questions the naive, literal level of language and image in order to expose its more shadowy, metaphorical significance.

Analysis of archetypal structures [Kugler continues] and the phenomenological amplification of images has characterized archetypal criticism from the 1920s to the mid-1960s, especially in the early work of John Thorburn (1925), Maud Bodkin ([1934] 1963), and Herbert Read (1967). (For a sampling see Hopper & Miller 1967.) Jungian theory extends into the influential writings of Northrop Frye (1957) and Leslie Fiedler (1960) and, in general, the whole school of "myth criticism."

2. Second-phase psychoanalysis (ego-psychology).

Freud's reasons for the shift
structural hypothesis: id, ego, superego
principle of multiple function (four-pole model)
autonomous ego functions: primary; secondary
defense mechanisms: projection, repression, undoing, etc.
aggressive/death instinct (Eros and Thanatos)

a.   Freud himself

Particularly important in second-phase psychoanalysis for
literary studies were the enlarged conception of defense, the
increased interest in early, pre-oedipal child development, and the
structural hypothesis of id, ego, and superego. Freud had mostly
ceased writing on literature by 1923. Even so, some of his earlier
works illustrate what his second-phase writing on literature might
have been like—his studies of jokes and humor, the legend of the
Medusa's Head, the theme of beauty's transience (an essay
prompted by Rilke), or the "uncanny" in ghost stories (see Strachey
1961). These more advanced writings all have less to do with the
author or with a character thought of as a real person, more with the
audience and an assumed collective response to a literary stimulus.

b.   Biography

In addition, biographical work based on second-phase (and
first-phase) psychoanalysis continues to the present by such biog-
raphers as Leon Edel, Justin Kaplan, Bernard Meyer, Norman
Fruman, Cynthia Wolff, and many others. Often, it is difficult to
detect a biographer's theoretical framework since the best writers
follow Edel's advice and avoid psychoanalytic jargon. Second-phase

psychobiography represented a marked improvement over first-phase. Where the first-phase biographer (Bonaparte, for example) tended to reduce adult achievement to childhood problems, a biographer using second-phase theory could show how the work of the adult both grew from *and coped with* crises recognizable in the childhood of the artist.

    c.   Criticism and theory

    Second-phase psychoanalytic theory made a more powerful poetics possible. Otto Rank, although by this time he had broken with Freud, developed the role of art in fantasies of immortality. Ernst Kris and Charles Mauron were able to integrate the new ego-psychology of multiple defenses into studies of the writing process. Mauron in particular related particular styles of defense to special, personal styles of writing. Ella Freeman Sharpe (1950) and Robert Rogers (1978) showed how the new theories could explicate the psychological function of metaphors and other poetic language.

    Kris, Simon Lesser, and Norman Holland used ego psychology to study the response to literary texts (still an assumed and collective response). Reflecting the new complexity in the theory of defenses, Kris treated the creation of and response to literature as "regression in the service of the ego" (1952). Lesser showed how literature makes differing appeals to id, ego, and superego (1957), and Robert Waelder demonstrated the same for the visual arts (1965). Marshall Bush (1967) and Pinchas Noy (1979) showed the importance of the ego to understanding literary forms; Angus Fletcher its importance for understanding genre (1964). Holland (1968) developed a model of literature as a fantasy modified by poetic forms (analogous to psychological defenses) toward a meaning. Where first-phase psychoanalytic critics felt they could analyze only persons, either writers or characters, these second-phase critics could use the new theories of defense to consider pure forms, like lyric poetry and nonfiction prose. They were able to extend psychoanalytic criticism, then, beyond literature and movies to the visual arts (Gombrich 1954; Ehrenzweig 1967; Fuller 1980), even to abstract forms (Andersen 1971; Kutash 1982), or music (Noy 1966-67; Feder et al. 1989). The anthologies by Ruitenbeek (1964), the Manheims (1966), or Tennenhouse (1976) provide good samples of second-phase psychoanalytic criticism. Skura (1981) represents a bridge between the strong scientism of second-phase psychoanalytic criticism and a more fluid sense of both criticism and psychoanalysis as related processes.

3. Third-phase psychoanalysis.

    a.   Psychosocial theory:

        epigenetic ground plan
        life stages
        psychosocial identity

    Although Erik Erikson's theories have greatly influenced political and historical thought in English-speaking countries, his teaching has had much less influence on Continental psychoanalysis (notably French) or literary criticism and theory. But see Franzosa 1973; Mazlish 1970; Noland 1979; and Lebeaux 1977, as well as Erikson's own studies in 1976 of George Bernard Shaw and Bergman's film, *Wild Strawberries*. Erikson's ideas have affected literature-and-psychology more as a matter of tone, encouraging literary critics to do less by way of an "originology" or "id-psychology," more in terms of the adaptive, ego-syntonic function of literature for its author. His famous essay on Freud's Irma dream (1968) encouraged attention to the manifest content of the dream, and this corresponds to second-phase literature-and-psychology's emphasis on literary form.

b.   Object-relations theory:

Arising out of the theories of Melanie Klein as revised by the London "middle school" of psychoanalysis, object-relations theory replaced Freud's instinctual-biological grounding of human motivation (Hughes 1989). (By *object*, of course, the psychoanalyst means "significant other," usually another person—parent, child, lover—but occasionally a thing.) Instead of imagining the human infant developing because it is propelled from within or behind, as it were, by a series of physiological urges, the object-relations school sees the developing child as creating and being created by its relations with mother, father, siblings, and playmates. Then, as in all psychoanalytic theory, the themes of the child persist, expressed in new modes, in the adult. In particular, both theory and observation indicate a crucial period early in life when the child felt it was not yet separate from its mother. Holland (1968) was able to show how this early experience could explain our feeling of being "absorbed" by literature later in life.

While the object-relations school as a whole has had an important influence on theory and therapy in England and America, only the writings of the pediatrician-psychoanalyst D. W. Winnicott, especially the *transitional object* and *potential space*, have had much influence on literary thought. Winnicott imagined the relationship between mother and child as a potential space, a space in which the "nursing couple" are not differentiated, and in which various transitional processes could take place, creating the capacity for illusion, play, and creativity in later life. Similarly, a transitional object is a teddy bear or security cloth that the child uses to alleviate the stress of separation and individuation from the mother. Such an object both is itself and is-not-but-merely-represents the mother or other significant object. It can comfort, yet it is, finally, only a thing. The transitional object serves as a prototype for all situations later in life when we use symbolisms to sustain ourselves. It is the forerunner of all important values and possessions, including works of art.

These ideas have influenced literary theory. In particular, as Murray Schwartz has shown (1975), Winnicott's concepts enable us to understand how a literary work feels both "in here" and "out there." It is, precisely, a transitional object in potential space (see also Bollas 1987; Grolnick & Barkin 1978). This way of thinking about the relationship between a reader and a text provides an important dimension to reader-response criticism (see b-i. below). Moreover, the theoretical move prescribed by the object-relations school, away from instinct and toward human relationships, has led to an important new approach to Shakespeare, a reading of the kinds of relationships in which his imagination works (see the Schwartz & Kahn anthology [1980]). Similarly, it opens up an approach to the visual arts in terms of the kinds of human styles and relationships represented (Fuller 1980; Milner 1957). Increased attention to the relationships of the first year of life coincides with the investigation of infants' and children's cognitive skills and ties this branch of psychoanalytic criticism to some current work in cognitive psychology (see h).

b-i. Modern Jungian criticism:

Here again, psychoanalysis and archetypal psychology touch. Winnicott's interest in the potential space between artist and work of art and between work of art and audience finds an echo in the work of James Hillman (1975, 1983). Hillman used something implicit in Jung's thinking to expand his clinical insights to a phenomenological study of imagination and language. Just as Winnicott uses free associations to unfold the potential space, so Hillman uses images. Paul Kugler has contributed another summary:

The most influential figure in the reformulation of archetypal criticism is Jungian psychoanalyst James Hillman. To extend Jungian psychology beyond clinical practice to a study of Western imagination, Hillman calls for a "post-analytic consciousness" committed to an articulation of the "poetic basis of mind." Hillman's phenomenological view of mind holds fantasy images to be the means by which consciousness and self-consciousness are possible and through which the world is imagined. Work with images, whether in therapeutic, cultural, or literary analysis, has become as much work on the process of seeing as on the object seen.

The shift from Jung to Hillman may perhaps be best illustrated in their differing approaches to alchemy. Where Jung writes an "objective" and "empirical" psychology of alchemy, Hillman tries instead to provide an experiential closeness to the alchemical images and tropes themselves. In writing about "silver and the white earth," Hillman intends his writing, like a poem, to bear traces of "silver," to become a "silver mine," unearthing and performing the images' tropological structure. The metaphor of silver "author-izes" the actual style of writing and internal logic of the text. As a mode of psychological criticism Hillman's new archetypal psychology assumes a literary work brings with it the very hermeneutics (imagos and tropes) by which it can be interpreted.

Kugler himself further developed the interrelation between alchemy and the poetic dimension of language (1982). He focused primarily on the interrelation between consciousness, language (texts), and imagos. Consciousness is continually being imagined (imaged, in-formed) by the metaphors in the very text it is writing or reading. Other modern Jungian critics have connected their psychol-

ogy to Heideggerian philosophy, deconstructionism, and notions of
nothingness and emptiness from Zen Buddhism, but they would take
us far afield.

    c.   Identity theory:

        primary identity
        identity principle
        identity theme
        DEFT
        relation to perception, object relations, reading—ARC
        "Delphi" teaching

    In 1961 Heinz Lichtenstein drew on third-phase psycho-
analysis's concern with the early relation of mother to child to conclude that human identity was established in that relationship and
could thereafter be read, like music, as a theme (a way of being the
child for this mother) and lifelong variations on that theme. One
could thus show in detail the thematic relationship between a
writer's life history and life style and literary style, as Lichtenstein
did with Thomas Chatterton (1977, ch. 10). Subsequently, Holland
showed how personal style (or identity) controlled the actual (as
opposed to the assumed) response to literature (1975a, b, 1988) and
to jokes (1982). Identity thus became an important theme in reader-
response criticism. In the "Delphi" seminars Holland, Schwartz, and
some of their students showed how one could use students' reading
and writing styles to explore personal identity in the classroom (Holland & Schwartz 1975; Holland 1977, 1978). Holland has also shown
how Lichtenstein's identity theory provides a bridge between psychoanalysis and cognitive psychology (1985, 1988).

    d.   Third force psychology:

real self
hierarchy of basic needs
self-actualization vs. self-alienation
world openness vs. embeddedness
transparency, congruence, spontaneity
authoritarian vs. humanistic conscience
interpersonal and intrapsychic strategies of defense
relation to Freudian theory

In the United States, some literary critics have built on the work of Karen Horney, whose theories reflect this second-phase psychoanalytic interest in defensive patterns and object relations. By accenting early childhood, libidinal phases, and sexuality less than other psychoanalytic critics, third force psychological critics (those, for example, in Bernard Paris's 1986 collection) have been able to write more realistically about authors and characters. Third-force criticism has added importantly to mimetic criticism, the treatment of literary events and characters as imitations (in Aristotle's sense) of real people.

e.   "French Freud" —is primarily Lacan:

the mirror stage
the signifier-signified relation and its *glissement*
desire and demand
the Real, the Imaginary, the Symbolic
the penis/phallus
nom du père

Central to Lacan's theory is an idea that has permeated French thought since World War II, namely, that the self is a "psychologizing," reactionary fiction. His thought colored by this bias, Lacan renders the self as split and de-centered. Conscious and unconscious are not just discontinuous but opposed.

The split begins in the so-called mirror stage posited by Lacan, a primary moment of alienation (related to Freud's early papers on splitting in the ego). The infant sees a unified image in a mirror and seeks to be that unrealizable ideal. But the child is in fact fragmented, created by the desires of its parents, and living in the alien linguistic system created by its culture. The second important moment for the developing child comes when it enters that linguistic world in Lacan's version of the oedipus complex. The child's pre-oedipal relation to its mother is *imaginary* (i.e., conducted in images, pre-verbal). As that dyadic relation becomes a triad including the father, the father introduces the principle of law, the name of the father, *le nom du père*. *Le nom du père* involves the linguistic cuts or "differences" that in Saussure's linguistics "signify" meanings. Hence Lacan equates *le nom du père* with castration in the classical oedipus complex.

With Lacan, as with Saussure, signifiers (words) simply signify as a lamp emits light. Hence, says Lacan, because we cannot control language, we cannot say what we mean. Nothing is as it seems. Every intellectual discourse runs contrary to unconscious truth. Ego psychology is wrong in trying to ally the self with the ego. For Lacan, then, the ego is the carrier of neurosis and self-deception. Therapy should aim, not to strengthen the ego (as in American ego-psychology) but to recognize the split, de-centered self, which is "the truth of the subject."

This kind of thinking appeals strongly to intellectuals because culture and language (at which intellectuals are adept) replace the biological models of classical and second-phase psychoanalysis. The mind is determined by language, not by organs of the body or brain and not by the object-relations of British theory. For therapy, Lacan substitutes a search for truth, which he called "science," a science far more like linguistics or philosophy than neurology or psychology. He stands for rebellion against the International Psycho-Analytic Association, the American ego-psychologists, the ego, and indeed the very idea of free will or an autonomous self. Lacan sees all of them as adaptations to culture, when the truth is that the individual is alienated from language, culture, and, most generally, the Other. These have structured the individual's own unconscious, which is opposed to the conscious ego. Lacan therefore proclaims that psychoanalysis must subvert every kind of intellectual establishment. All this, of course, has made Lacan a favorite of the intellectual establishment.

Lacan wrote in an avowedly obscure style. In effect, he used the materials of first-phase psychoanalysis (the oedipal paradigm, the phallus, castration) as the language in which to express third-phase concerns like self, object relations, psychosis, or cognitive functions (Schwartz & Willbern 1982, 215-216). As a result much Lacanian literary theory simply tries to explicate Lacan (see ch. 3, 3.e).

Nevertheless, so far as literature-and-psychology is concerned, Lacan rested important psychoanalytic ideas on analyses of Poe's "Purloined Letter" (1956b) and *Hamlet* (1959), and his commentary on Joyce is interesting (1987). Lacan's psychoanalysis entered the American literary world in an issue of *Yale French Studies* punningly called "French Freud" (Mehlman 1972; see also Felman 1982, 1987). Many Lacanian critics have begun to work on specific texts (Bersani 1977, 1986; Felman 1978; Hartman 1978; Davis 1981; Silhol 1984), although much Lacanian writing is "theory" halfway between psychology and literary theory. Grimaud's 1982 survey is particularly apposite. Current criticism appears in the journals *Littoral* and *Ornicar?*, and current bibliography of both literary and psychological

materials in *Newsletter of the Freudian Field*. Lacan's own writings
are still being published (1975-). A helpful bibliographical note is
that in Ragland-Sullivan (1986).

Lacan has proved highly influential in film criticism, where
Christian Metz (1982), Stephen Heath (1981), and many other
theorists have applied Lacanian psychoanalysis to articulate the ways
audiences are "sutured" into films through the gaps created by edit-
ing. The anthologies by Nichols (1976), Mast and Cohen (1985), and
Ann Kaplan (1989) offer a sampling of this line of work and Andrew
(1984, ch. 8) and Gabbard and Gabbard (1987, ch. 7) provide surveys. Lacan has also proved influential in feminism (see 3-g).

Lacanian psychoanalysis meshes with the claims of such French
thinkers as Roland Barthes, Michel Foucault, or Jacques Derrida,
who treat language as an active, autonomous system, and the
speaker as passive (Wright 1984, pts. 3 and 4). Lacan's de-centered
self leads to the impossibility of arriving at textual meaning—another
major premise of postmodern thought. Lacan is therefore widely
read in literary circles, more so than earlier versions of literature-
and-psychoanalysis. Paradoxically, however, this version of psychoanalysis minimizes the importance of the actual free associating person on whom the entire edifice of psychoanalysis rests.

That is one of my three objections to this version of psychoanalysis: the assumption that the self is disunified because conscious
and unconscious are *opposed*. That is only an assumption, a bias or
prejudice, really. There is no evidence for it, neither experimental
evidence from psychologists nor clinical evidence from first- or
second-phase psychoanalysts. How, for example, does it fit the well-
known experience of sublimation? This claim, that conscious and
unconscious self are opposed, is only one example of a basic pattern
in Lacan's thinking. He characteristically renders as either-or or as
an opposition what had previously made sense as both-and or an

interaction: conscious vs. unconscious, self vs. not-self, unity vs. conflict, science vs. unconscious truth, and so on. Finally, Lacan's
system as a whole rests on Saussure's linguistic principle of signifying. Chomsky's work, however, has rendered Saussure's linguistics
weak and inadequate. Nevertheless "signifying" remains the basic
principle of causality in Lacanian psychoanalysis.

    f.   Narcissism theory:

    the "self-object" (Kohut) or self-object-affect cluster
      (Kernberg)
    narcissism vs. object-libido
    dual development
    grandiose self
    idealized parent-imago
    sense of cohesion of self

    In the United States, psychoanalysts have become increasingly
concerned with the treatment of so-called borderline personalities,
illnesses characteristic of late twentieth-century individuals and
rooted in the pre-oedipal relationship of the infant to its earliest
caregiver. The writings of Heinz Kohut have been particularly
influential in the development of new thories of empathy and narcissism. Kohut goes so far as to suggest stages of development of self-
esteem parallel to the classical psychoanalytic stages of development
of libido (oral, anal, and so on). Otto Kernberg has put forward a
concept of the child developing through clusters of self-object-affect
relations. For both writers the concept of a self-object with whom
the infant or adult may merge is important and may provide a pattern for relationships to literature. These ideas are just beginning to
percolate literary circles, but there has already been one anthology

of criticism (Layton & Shapiro 1986) based on the theory of narcissism.

    g.   Feminist psychoanalysis:

        patriarchal society
        differential parenting
        rewriting Freud
        Lacanian approaches

    A particularly vigorous current in late twentieth-century
literature-and-psychology is feminist psychoanalytic criticism (see,
for example, the collections by Barr & Feldstein 1989 and Feldstein
& Roof 1989). It began in the 1960s with Friedan's social (1963) and
Millett's literary (1970) polemics. Both strenuously attacked first-
and second-phase psychoanalysis (especially American ego-
psychology). Psychoanalysts, they pointed out, claim a scientific
validity for penis envy and Freud's deprecating remarks about
women. Freud, however, failed to acknowledge any influence on his
ostensibly objective scientific views from his personal and social
biases. Psychoanalysts take the male psyche as a norm. Psychoanalysts treat differences between men and women as women's
lacks. While acknowledging the truth of these charges, Mitchell
(1974) was more informed about psychoanalysts after Freud. She
opened, in effect, negotiations between feminism and psychoanalysis
by insisting on the usefulness of even a patriarchal psychology for
understanding the male-dominated society women face.
    This first round drew two issues between the two disciplines.
How valid is the psychoanalytic account of woman? How much
force has psychoanalysis as a science? The first question even psychoanalysts concede: the psychoanalytic account of woman needs
(and by 1989 has received) revision. To the other question I see two

general approaches. One, roughly Anglo-American, accepts psycho-analysis as a scientific psychology but updates it. The other, roughly Franco-American, substitutes Lacan's concept of psychoanalysis as language or narrative and thereby reduces the claims of psycho-analysis.

The Anglo-American approach can be more psychology than literary criticism. Its ancestor would be Horney's early papers (collected in 1967) critiquing the psychoanalytic account of woman within the framework of psychoanalysis. Chodorow's powerful rewriting of second-phase psychoanalysis in the light of English object-relations theory (1978) provides a more sophisticated account of both male and female development than first- or second-phase psychoanalysis. She thus gives a basis for feminist readings of texts (Gilbert & Gubar 1979, 1988- ; Garner et al. 1985; Lenz et al. 1980), readings that emphasize the role of gender in the process of creation and in the finished text. Similarly the revised psychoanalytic account of woman gives theory for distinguishing female readers from male in reader-response criticism. Gardiner (1976) and Fetterley (1978) note the difficulty of the woman reader reading under male notions of how and what to read. Flynn and Schweickart's collection (1986) gives feminist and female responses and theory (including cognitive research) to explain them.

The Franco-American approach is more abstract. Where the Anglo-Americans address real readers and situations, the Franco-Americans polarize feminist questions into body and language. Some conclusions come from "biological essentializing"—reasoning from male and female anatomy. Others focus on the general idea of man's (dominant) language—abstract, scientific, competitive—as opposed to woman's language (see, for example, Marks & de Courtivron 1980 or Gelfand & Hules 1985 or Moi 1987.) Social critics in this group set the question of language in readings of society, particularly seen as monotheistic, capitalist, and patriarchal (Irigaray 1974, 1977; Kristeva 1986). In a more literary vein, this school sometimes rereads and rewrites Freud as if he were a literary text (Cixous 1975). Others in this group privilege hysteria as woman speaking against patriarchal society and medicine (Bernheimer & Kahane 1985; Cixous & Clément 1986). Strong feminist film criticism has evolved from this line of thought: studies of the patriarchal interests of traditional, commercial cinema; the privileging of the male gaze and the positioning of woman as gazed-at (Mulvey 1975; de Lauretis 1984); the allaying of male anxieties associated with the female body (Mulvey 1975; see also Kristeva 1980).

Feminists have found in psychoanalytic psychology both a challenge and a resource. I consider myself a feminist and am in sympathy with much of this writing. Out of necessity, however, much of it shades off into social rather than literary criticism and is beyond my purview here. As for what is strictly lit-and-psych, I strongly prefer the Anglo-American school for two reasons. First, although I share the postmodern idea that psychoanalysis and science and history and biography are all narratives, one nevertheless has to recognize that they are different kinds of narratives. Their makers play by different rules. Psychoanalysis, because it claims to be a science (Holland 1985, part 3), has to touch down to reality and evidence in ways that a novelist need not. One cannot just revise psychoanalysis as if it were a story—not and keep it psychoanalysis. Second, as the Franco-American school pursues rhetoric, I believe they create a paper feminism. They lose sight of the real oppression of woman in the professions, in social and economic structures, and in everyday life. In other words, I would extend to this branch of feminist thought my general objection to the Lacanian conversion of psychological causes and effects into mere language. Both these failings seem to me classic instances of the omnipotence of thought that plagues literary critics, philosophers, and psychoanalysts (see p. 60). Nevertheless feminist criticism in both its branches has invigorated and reformed the whole discipline of psychoanalysis.

h. Cognitive Psychology

There were I. A. Richards's (1924, 1929) and Morse Peckham's (1965) somewhat eclectic use of psychology, an occasional nod to a gestalt psychologist like Kurt Koffka (1935), or a mention of Jean Piaget's work on the development of play and symbolic thought (Beard 1969). Mostly, however, academic psychology did not begin to attract the attention of literary critics or theorists until the 1970s. Then cognitive science simply exploded (Gardner 1985). *Poetics* (- 1971-) was the first journal to provide a forum on theory for both literary scholars and scientists of *les sciences de l'homme* and spurred three other journals, *Spiel* (1982-), *Empirical Studies of the Arts* (1983-), and *Metaphor and Symbolic Activity* (1986-). First, Russian formalists, then French structuralists and German text-grammarians, and now many different kinds of literary theorists have begun to draw on artificial intelligence, developmental and cognitive psychology, and other subfields of "the mind's new science" (Gardner's 1985 title), cognitive sciences that deal with poems, stories, humor, metaphor—in general, symbolic activities.

For example, *Metaphors We Live By* (1980) by cognitive linguist George Lakoff and philosopher Mark Johnson shows that we often think in a logic of metaphor, an argument they each greatly extended in separate books in 1987: this metaphorical logic tells us a great deal about the way our minds work. Similarly, Schank and Abelson's work on computers' understandings of situations demonstrates that much of remembering and thinking functions according to storylike scenarios (1977). Together such research suggests that if metaphors

and stories underlie the structure and functioning of the human conceptual system, then a psychology of literature and the rhetorical
phenomena of everyday life must be central to any theory of the
mind (Beaugrande 1980). We need to understand how our expecta-
tions create suspense or interest in both real and fictional story-
worlds as we imagine impending catastrophes or alternative roads
not taken. These hypotheses do not come from the story alone (Jose
& Brewer 1984; Beaugrande & Colby 1979). They are learned and
internalized as part of culture, as shown by those, like Howard
Gardner and other workers at Harvard's Project Zero, who study
how children develop artistic ability and the capacity to formulate
hypotheses about stories and pictures (Perkins & Leondar 1977). A
similar process applies to music (Davies 1978). Likewise, David
Bordwell has shown how we respond to films by constructing them
through such schemata (1985), powerfully extending a very early
insight by Hugo Münsterberg (1916).

In general, from a cognitive psychologist's perspective, 1980s
literary theory often rests on static ideas of "signifier-signified" or
"content" that do not accord with the active processes by which
people perceive and understand and the dynamic, "illogical"
processes by which they think and feel. The cultural codes and
canons people use to perceive things fit neatly into psychoanalysis's
understanding of the role of the individual in making and responding
to literature and the other arts. Putting this understanding into practice is the challenge for literature-and-cognitive-psychology.
Grimaud (1984) suggests a possible synthesis as does Holland (1988,
1985).

i.   Reader-Response Criticism:

By "reader-response criticism," I mean criticism or theory that
focuses on the reader or audience and their experiencing of a text.

Reader-response criticism, at least in its current American version, touches on several of the methodologies of psychoanalysis's "psychology of the self."

In a sense, of course, all literary criticism began and remains reader-response criticism because literary theory always involves a model of reading, even if it remains tacit. Plato's ban on poets, the opposite critical claim (for the moral efficacy of literature), Aristotle's catharsis, Longinus's sublime, and modern concepts like Brecht's alienation-effect or the Russian formalists' "defamiliarization" all rest on assumptions about reader-response. In a more specific sense, however, reader-response criticism refers to a group of critics who explicitly study, not a text, but readers reading a text.

Reader-response criticism, in this specific sense, emerged from 1967-70 in America and Germany (see the surveys by, in chronological order, Purves & Beach 1972; Segers 1975; Suleiman & Crosman 1980; Tompkins 1980; Holub 1984; Freund 1987). Important predecessors would include I. A. Richards, who in 1929 analyzed a group of Cambridge undergraduates' misreadings of poems, and Louise Rosenblatt, whose 1937 book insisted on the unique relationship of each reader to aesthetic texts. In opposition, a famous article by Wimsatt and Beardsley in 1954 attacked the "affective fallacy." To evaluate a poem in terms of its emotional effect, they said, was to confuse the poem with its result. They thus assumed an "objective" text, separate from its reader but entailing certain appropriate responses, and this became a cornerstone of the "New Criticism."

The reader-response critic holds exactly the opposite view. A "text" involves a psychological process in which author and reader interact through a physical text. Critics often claim "objectivity," but it is an illusion. One cannot read a text except by the processes by which we perceive texts (and they are driven by our sense of the text's relation to our feelings and values, including our ideas of how one ought to read a text). For the reader-response critic as for the modern physicist probing the atom, the answer you get depends on the question you ask.

Within this general position, critics (primarily in Germany and the United States) have developed different versions of reader-response theory, with the fundamental difference being between those who regard individual differences in responses as important and those who do not. One group of reader-response critics (largely Continental) envisages a mostly uniform response to a text (with unimportant personal variations). The other (an Anglo-American group) sees individual variations as large enough to show the reader in control at every point. The former say what is common in different readers' readings results from the text, while those who see the reader in control explain what is common as resulting from common strategies and tactics for reading, individually applied by different readers. By and large, German and other Continental critics tend to use generic and philosophical (nonpsychological) concepts of the reader. The Americans tend to use actual individuals, sometimes the critic's own self (Fish), sometimes students and others free associating (Bleich, Holland). As a result most American reader-response critics (but few of the Continental) draw heavily on psychology, often psychoanalytic psychology, since it addresses individuality.

Among the Americans, Bleich pioneered the study of the actual feelings and free associations of readers as early as 1967, and he has applied his findings in four books both theoretically to model the reading process and practically to reform the classroom teaching of literature (1975, 1977, 1978, 1988; see also Grant 1987). After examining the real responses of real readers, Holland in 1975 gave up his second-phase account of the literary process (see 2-c) for a third-phase model. A personal identity (defined as a theme and variations) *uses* the physical text and invariable codes (such as the shapes of letters) and variable canons (different critical values, for example) to build a response both like and unlike other responses (see also 1986b and c and 1988). In earlier writings, Fish used "the" reader to examine sequential, word-by-word responses to complex sentences. Since 1976, however, he too has emphasized the real differences among real readers using reading tactics endorsed by different schools of criticism and by the literary professoriate. The journal *Reader* publishes a succession of articles using reader-response theory in pedagogy.

The Anglo-American reader-response critics displace meaning, structure, and the like from something "in" a text to a psychological process and hence require a psychology. From the outset, psychoanalytic psychology has provided critics like Bleich, Holland, or Schwartz with techniques for analyzing the language of individual responders. In the 1970s and 1980s, cognitive psychology, psycholinguistics, and neuroscience have provided increasingly powerful and detailed models for the way readers read (Rumelhart 1977; Anderson et al. 1977; Dillon 1978; Sternberg 1985). In general, psychologists of reading and those who teach reading to illiterates or schoolchildren conclude, like reader-response critics, that readers make meaning (Spiro et al. 1980; Smith 1982; Meek et al. 1982, 1983, 1985; Crowder 1982; Taylor & Taylor 1983). Further, most late-twentieth-century psychology of perception supports the reader-response idea that perceivers construct what they perceive. Hence reader-response criticism can readily be extended to other arts like cinema (Holland 1986b) or painting (as with art historian E. H. Gombrich) or to the perception of events (as in the historiography of Hayden White or the philosophy of science of those feminist philosophers who envision a science that acknowledges the involvement of the scientist—Harding & Hintikka 1983). Reader-response critics often share the concerns of feminist critics because they value readings of a text not available to a white, male, middle-class, Western reader. Hence reader-response criticism leads to exploration of "gender and reading" (Flynn & Schweickart 1986).

In short, reader-response criticism touches on a variety of themes in third-phase psychoanalysis: personal identity; the feminist critique of psychoanalysis; the unconscious use of linguistic codes (Lacan); the spectator or the "suture" of cinema; cognitive science, notably personal styles of knowing and perceiving; and the Winnicottian blurring of boundaries between self and other, in here and out there. In many ways, reader-response criticism is, in the world of literary criticism, the most practical embodiment of the basic psychoanalytic insight that all knowledge is personal knowledge.

5

Epilogue

IN SOMETHING called an "epilogue," I am obviously going to be even more personal than in the more dispassionate "guide" that preceded it. I want to set down some closing thoughts on the "truth" of psychoanalysis. "Truth," what is "real," what we can all believe and rely on—these issues matter to me, more perhaps than to others. They form basic themes in my identity (perhaps because of a childhood with a lot of unreality in it—or things I wished were unreal and didn't really know whether they were or not).

At any rate, this concern for what is true or real colors my presentation even of something so ostensibly impersonal as a list of readings. It must, for the fundamental truth that psychoanalysis teaches is, All knowledge is personal knowledge. Hence this *Guide*—to enable you to have personal knowledge, at least of the psychoanalytic literature. I cannot give you the even more important personal knowledge of the psychoanalytic experience.

But if psychoanalysis teaches us that all knowledge is personal, how can I speak of the "truth" of psychoanalysis? Even though I believe the truth of what I am about to say, that very truth says it is opinion and belief, not "truth" in the conventional, absolute sense. This is the postmodern paradox psychoanalysis leads us into and leaves us in.

It is the sort of paradox with which modern literary and philosophical writers about psychoanalysis like to toy. Playing with verbal paradoxes leads to an abstract, philosophical kind of psychoanalysis. Few concepts are grounded in clinical experience or experimental observation.

I associate this philosophizing of psychoanalysis largely with Lacan's teaching and its various offshoots. They render psychoanalysis merely language. Phalluses, fathers, castration, loss, the oppression of women, psychological determinism itself, all become simply words. This mental tactic seems to me a classic example of what psychoanalysts term *the omnipotence of thoughts* or *magical thinking*. That is, we sometimes attribute to thoughts (or language or symbols) the powers of real things, and we exaggerate those powers to magical proportions. Think of the way people get agitated about flags, crucifixes, or sexual pictures. Think of the power or eroticism or emotion they attribute to these symbols, although they are, after all, only things. Literary people and philosophers attribute magical powers to language, Lacanians attribute magical powers to "signifying," superpatriots and politicians to flags, ayatollahs to novels, fundamentalists to pornography. Magical thinking is an error we all easily stumble into, but that is no reason to dive into it eagerly, headfirst.

To be sure, Lacanians are correct to insist that psychoanalysis takes place in language. And we postmodernists are correct to insist that we cannot perceive apart from the symbolic structures in our heads. That does not mean, as many literary people seem to write, that these symbolic structures have the same kind of hard-edged force as solids "out there" in the world beyond our fingertips and our skulls.

I reject a philosophical, really a magical, version of psycho-analysis, then, because I think it confuses words and things. I want some proof of what psychoanalysis asserts, something the mind can rest on more securely than the reasons one might believe, say, Nietzsche or Saint Augustine.

I am not, however, advocating the opposite extreme: High Church New York Psychoanalytic Institute orthodoxy as exposed in Janet Malcolm's book. The delightful double entendre in its title, *Psychoanalysis: The Impossible Profession*, says it all. Nor do I advo-cate the avant-garde of the International Psycho-Analytic Associa-tion. All too often, in discussions both by conservative and third-phase psychoanalysts, terms become almost metaphysical, they have moved so far from testable experience. I am thinking of Winnicott's "false self," Kohut's "empathy," Waelder's "ego pleasure," Hart-mann's "will-processes," Khan's "space of illusion," Lacan's "materiality"—indeed all too many of Lacan's concepts. Others, I know, find such terms usable and useful. I, however, would be hard put to decide whether a given action by a patient or therapist fits within these terms or not.

As you might expect, given my predilection for the "true" and the "real," the psychoanalysis I respect rests on observation and test-ing. Even with psychoanalytic writers whose ideas I otherwise admire and readily work with (Winnicott, for example), when their terms cease to be the starting-point for some actual test, I become uncertain and troubled. I need some feedback through the real world. I distrust any version of psychoanalysis that gets too far away from the actual experience of couch, clinic, or laboratory. I fear that psychoanalysis, either in its most traditional form or its most radical, postmodern versions, will turn into a twentieth-century scholasticism, in which not-very-monkish monks write ever more abstruse commentaries on a canon of received texts. The omnipotence of thoughts again.

I want to return to what seem to me a core of ideas, strongly evidenced over decades of actual psychoanalytic experience. I would like to start out again from such a core. The psychoanalysis I admire is a science, albeit of a very paradoxical kind. It is paradoxical because it redefines what science is (but more of that anon).

I know there is a canard circulated around intellectual circles that psychoanalysis is untested and untestable. It is high time someone pointed out that this notion is purely and simply false. There is a large body of psychological research that does just that—tests psychoanalytic ideas, confirming and sometimes disconfirming them. Indeed, the list of books *surveying* this research is itself fairly long. I have included two of the more recent in section 0-c of this Topical Outline, but one can easily enough do one's own survey by looking up "psychoanalysis" in *Psychological Abstracts*. There is also an important annual volume, *Empirical Studies of Psychoanalytic Theories*, edited by Joseph Masling, whose bibliographies hold a wealth of such materials.

It is simply not true that psychoanalysis is untested or untestable. It is true, of course, that, when subjected to experiment or "empirical testing," not all psychoanalytic ideas have proved out. Happily, Freud's boyish theories on women do not pass muster. Neither does much of "metapsychology" or many of the impressionistic memories and language of psychoanalysts. The terms I have complained of, which cannot be defined or observed, of course, do not get tested. Nevertheless, I can put my mind around a core of psychoanalytic thought that supplies testable hypotheses, which have been tested against the real world. This core feels like a firm set of ideas for psychological and literary work, strong enough even for a materialist like me.

What do I think constitutes that core? Out of the immense technical literature psychoanalysis produces—and if you have ever attended meetings of, say, the American Psychoanalytic Association, you know that, once out from behind the couch, psychoanalysts who have been muffling themselves hour after hour in self-imposed silence can get very verbose indeed—out of that immense psychoanalytic literature, I would pick six firm markers by which to navigate in thinking about the human mind.

First and foremost is *free association*. I think it is Freud's most fundamental discovery. You could even argue that it is the *only* thing Freud discovered. All the rest followed more or less automatically once people began free associating.

Free association means saying, without regard for relevance or shame, whatever comes to mind. If a patient free associates in connection with a symptom, a dream, a slip in speech, a lapse of memory, or an error in writing, the patient will become aware (against resistance) of some previously unconscious wish. Indeed, as therapy ceased to be bound to the particular symptom or dream or slip, it became clear that free association, just running along by itself so to speak, would *always* reveal a resisted latent or unconscious content underneath tolerated manifest or conscious behavior. Furthermore, what was revealed would be not only a wish or cluster of wishes (a fantasy) but also the defense mechanisms by which the patient shaped the unconscious material into consciously acceptable speech. Still further, one could interpret *any* acceptable speech in the same way. One could interpret the dreamer's account of a dream this way. One could interpret the literary critic's interpretation of a text as well. Both express unconscious wishes and largely unconscious defenses. That is, psychoanalytic clinical experience tells us about the kinds of wishes people are likely to have and the kinds of defenses they are likely to use to manage those wishes. If you look for wishes and defenses in a piece of language, you will find them.

What you are finding is "the" unconscious. (My quotation marks signal Freud's first-phase usage: the unconscious as a noun.) Often said to be Freud's fundamental discovery, it seems to me to follow from something still more fundamental: a way of getting at "the" unconscious. Freud showed us how to discover "the" unconscious through the language people choose. It is this speech of the mind, this language-ridden human animal's conscious words and actions yielding hitherto unconscious thoughts and feelings, that is the factual foundation of psychoanalysis.

Speech is as much a fact as any other sound—as our senses daily prove. The process of unconscious thoughts and feelings emerging through speech is a hypothesis confirmed every hour in any kind of "talking psychotherapy," whether it is psychoanalytic or not. This process is the truth that psychoanalysis tells in pulse and bone. If you have experienced it you know it is true. If you have not, it is harder, of course, to credit but no less provably true. One can demonstrate it by a variety of experimental techniques (hypnosis, for example, or further free association). Clinical validation of these unconscious processes rests on interpretation, to be sure. Nevertheless, one can compare different interpretations, and one can sift the better from the worse.

These, then, are two of my six basic markers for charting the mind: free association and the unknown, invisible thoughts *cum* feelings that free association reveals—"the" unconscious (in the language of the first phase). A third foundation for psychoanalysis is its account of child development. Improbable as that account often sounds, it seems to me, quite simply, proven—and for an odd and personal reason.

When I first tried applying psychoanalysis to literature, one thing utterly convinced me of its validity. Writers who could not possibly have read Freud would nevertheless demonstrate in their writings clusters of imagery that are described only in psychoanalysis. These clusters are the base of what psychoanalysts discover in therapy with adults about the fantasies and drives of children, the so-called psychoanalytic stages of child development. But you find anality in Ben Jonson (first noticed by Edmund Wilson), Molière, Nikolai Gogol, Charles Dickens, or Gerard Manley Hopkins. You find orality in Marlowe, Marvell, Keats, or George Bernard Shaw. You find phallic images and traits in Aristophanes or Apuleius or Boccaccio or Chaucer or Laurence Sterne or Mark Twain. And, of course, you find oedipal fantasies in almost any plot that involves a male-female triangle or sexual jealousy.

There was no way these writers could have read Freud and deliberately imitated his account of the childhood stages. Indeed, analysts themselves did not really spell out these clusters of imagery until the 1920s and after, and I think my 1968 book was the first to state them all in one place as literary occurrences.

These pre-Freudian imaginative writings seemed to me the strongest kind of evidence for the "developmental" point of view of psychoanalysis. They were proving what the psychoanalysts claimed: the persistence of childhood themes in the adult. They were *proving* it because these pre-Freudian writers were evidencing psychoanalytic themes they could not conceivably have imitated in a deliberate, studied way. Nor did the analysts developing these concepts refer to these writers as examples for their theories. This was a wholly independent corroboration.

Furthermore, because these themes involved many details within a given poem or story, not just a single image, they were more persuasive than the discovery of a "Freudian symbol" or a parapraxis or a pun here and there. Working with imagery convinced me that these clusters, and the childhood stages of development that defined them, had a psychological reality. What the psychoanalysts recovered in adult analyses and what they claimed to have observed in children, I found in literature. These things must be so.

Still further, I began to find these patterns of imagery in intellectual writings as well as imaginative: essays by Arnold or Mill, New Critical essays analyzing poetic texts (including my own criticism), and, inevitably, Freud's own writings. Finding unconscious fantasy materials in intellectual texts meant that conscious thought grew from unconscious roots. No matter how adult or abstruse what is being said, one can hear in it, using the "third ear" Freud and the first generation of analysts gave us, childhood. There is an unconscious dimension to *everything* we think or say, and we can reach it through analysis of the language we use. As you can imagine, this literary critic was *very* excited. All knowledge is personal knowledge.

The psychoanalytic account of child development thus makes my third, and crucial, navigational marker. For my next I go on to "character," a powerful second-phase concept. At first tied to childhood stages, one spoke of an "oral" or an "anal" or a "phallic" character. Then, as Freud's circle in the 1930s and later Anglo-American analysts formulated it, character was a person's habitual way of dealing with inner and outer reality. In the framework of ego-psychology, character was the ego's habitual way of dealing with the id, the superego, the repetition compulsion, and outer reality (see the Topical Outline 2-c). The important word is "habitual." At any given moment the ego is balancing competing demands from these four agencies. Character is the way it does so over and over again.

Interestingly (if parenthetically), the idea of "character" in this theoretical sense seems never to have entered French psychoanalysis. The term appears only as "character neurosis" in Daniel Lagache's pre-Lacan textbook of psychoanalysis (which went through ten editions from 1955 to 1971). Laplanche and Pontalis in their authoritative psychoanalytic dictionary (1968) oriented toward French psychoanalysis give, as the broadest sense, a dominance by one or another psychic agency (say, the superego or the ego-ideal). (What this leaves out is Waelder's "principle of multiple function.") Lacan, of course, does not use the concept.

This lack is one reason French psychoanalysis looks so different from English or American. It is all the more surprising because French classical literature brought the genre of the literary "character" to such a fine art. Perhaps it was in reaction to that neo-classical tradition that, after World War II, French intellectuals decided that an autonomous self was a bourgeois, capitalist fiction. Even mentioning "identity" or such concepts can get you into trouble among the French and their American disciples. Salons will be as effectively closed to you, wrote one of my French translators, as if you had ordered bourbon with your tournedos.

In the early days, psychoanalysts would simply speak of an "oral" character or an "anal" character. As psychoanalysis became more sophisticated, analysts would include in a description of character a person's preferred or habitual defense mechanisms. By defense mechanism in this context one can mean in the technical definition, a mental tactic applied rapidly, unconsciously, and automatically at a signal of danger. More generally, one might speak of defenses as coping mechanisms or adaptations, ways of dealing with outer as well as inner reality.

Like the fantasies of the childhood stages, defenses (or adaptations) became an immensely useful concept for me as a literary critic. I could see them in literary texts, and not just in the actions of realistic characters coping with the world. They corresponded to literary forms. Metaphor was like displacement. Irony was like reversal. Simile was a form of symbolization, as was metonymy. Omission was like denial. Parallel plots were like splitting or isolation. One could compare various literary maneuvers with the defenses described in various psychoanalytic handbooks. Moreover, a given writer would use one form or defense over and over again, in preference to others. One could describe a style psychoanalytically, then, not only in terms of content (characteristic fantasies) but also in terms of form (characteristic defenses).

Second-phase psychoanalysts, however, continued to think of a person's character as membership in a type or class: a diagnostic category (for example, paranoid or obsessional), a libidinal stage (oral or anal), or a preferred defense (denial, reversal, intellectualization). Even in that form the concept seems to me valid and useful. I think it is very like the literary critic's idea of "style." Style in literature is simply the character of a writing. One can speak of style as various types: pastoral or lyric or metaphysical or operatic. These types, like the psychoanalytic categories, will serve for a first approximation.

For a finer reading, however, the concept of a style should point not only to a type but also an individuality. Within the general type "pastoral," there is a Marlovian or a Marvellian or a Keatsian pastoral. Similarly, all three of these poets use clusters of images from the oral stage as described by psychoanalysts. They are oral types. As a literary critic, though, I want to be able to use psychoanalysis to describe them as individual styles or characters within the general type "oral."

I found a way to do that in Heinz Lichtenstein's 1961 version of *identity*. Lichtenstein posited an identity made up of a theme and variations, like a piece of music. Using this version of identity, one could describe an individual as an individual rather than a class, just as an account of a theme and its variations defines a unique piece of music. For Lichtenstein, identity is a life history rendered as an identity theme and a lifetime of variations on that theme.

Like characteristic defenses and character itself, the concept seems to me a useful guide. I have seen identities (personal themes and variations on those themes) over and over again: in writers, in students, in colleagues and administrators, and in politicians. I have seen identity in myself. Students in my classes regularly work with one another's identities. Ordinary, nonpsychoanalytic people speak readily of some act as being in or out of character, tacitly assuming a concept of identity. "There he goes again" is a famous political *mot*.

I must also confess that there are a great many people out there whom I have been unable to convince of identity in this sense. I do not believe they reject it because they have tried to apply it and found that it yielded no useful feedback. I think they reject the concept because they have a prejudice against it. For example, people see identity (correctly) as a form of "essentializing" or "thematizing," and current intellectuals think those are bad things. People think (incorrectly) that identity does not allow for personal change or novelty. People think the idea of identity is a capitalist, imperialist concept that supports some reactionary political position (for reasons that escape me). And so on. None of this do I find convincing.

What would unsettle my conviction would be a genuine effort to work with the concept that failed. If one does not choose to apply this hypothesis, if one believes, for example, that the human subject has been deconstructed (as many modern literary people claim), one will not, of course, see identity. That does not imply there is no such thing as identity, only that one has chosen not to look for it.

When I say I have seen the hypothesis of identity work, however, you should remember precisely what hypothesis has been tested. Strictly speaking, the hypothesis is that one *can* interpret a person as a theme and variations.

Unlike Lichtenstein, I do not wish to claim that an identity theme is "in" a person. Lichtenstein borrowed the concept of *imprinting* from animal studies. The best known examples are the goslings who grew up thinking Konrad Lorenz was their mother because he was there at the critical "imprinting" time after they hatched.

I do not wish to adopt Lichtenstein's idea of an identity theme "in" the person, even though there is increasing evidence of a growing and ungrowing in the infant mammalian brain that supports Lichtenstein's view. Experience carves out in the infant's changing brain particular synapses and pathways, those that the infant uses in the experiences it is having. As infants we learned, in Lichtenstein's phrase, to be the child for this particular mother (and father and culture). Our experience of doing so may well have wired an identity into our brains (Holland 1988).

Nevertheless, for me, the identity we can use to understand ourselves is not so much a structure in the mind as a way of interpreting a person as a theme and variations. Identity involves a paradox and paradoxical implications. If it is true that I can interpret any other human being as a theme and variations, then I can interpret their interpretations of things as a theme and variations. (We say, for example, that a given interpretation sounds like Dr. Johnson or Coleridge or Ihab Hassan or Walter Ong.) If so, then, you can do the same for me. You can see me (in this *Guide*, for example) interpreting literature or psychoanalysis or your identity in characteristic ways. That is, you can read my interpretations and values and beliefs as functions of my identity (gleaned perhaps from the first paragraph of this chapter). But in doing so you would be interpreting as a function of your own identity. Even if identity were "in" a person, by that very fact, you and I could not interpret such an identity except through our own identities. None of us can interpret or even perceive things except within our own identities as they operate the processes by which we interpret and perceive.

The concept of identity thus lets us see how we human beings, because we have personalities, are both enabled and limited by those personalities. We can only know in the style in which we know things. All knowledge is personal knowledge. We come back again to that fundamental psychoanalytic truth.

Identity, then, is a hypothesis I apply to interpret people. It is only one among many hypotheses we use to interpret the world, and in saying that I come to another of my navigational landmarks, namely, *feedback*. We perceive and interpret the world by a process of applying hypotheses and seeing what we get back as the world responds. This is not so much a psychoanalytic point of view as one firmly established in cognitive science. It is the psychologists who show us using feedback to perceive and know the world. Feedback dovetails, however, with psychoanalytic concepts like identity.

Our culture offers us a repertoire of such hypotheses with which to test and interpret the world. (Among them, of course, is the identity I see in other individuals.) The hypotheses we choose from that repertoire, the way we apply them, the way we interpret the results, and the way we feel about what we get back—all are parts of our feedback processes. All are aspects of our own personal identity. Identity is what governs the myriad kinds of feedback, both social and biological, that we use to see, to know, to remember, learn, move, in short, to live.

Feedback thus directs me to another psychoanalytic marker, Winnicott's concept of *potential space*. This, too, I find another firm point (even if it describes a blur). That is, Winnicott describes a space between infant and mother (and later, between adult self and other) in which "creative living" takes place. I understand that phrase by means of this concept of feedback. Feedback implies that the boundary between self and other is not a line or a thing or a place but a process. We are continually testing. We are therefore "between" inside and outside, past and future, inner self and "out there." So is potential space. Feedback implies, like potential space, an organism that is constantly testing and trying.

In infancy, our deepest preverbal being forms itself as we test out a geometry of human relationships and physical space. As infants (and as adults) we live in spaces of closeness, oneness, distance, presence, absence, and so on. Already, by the time a child begins to speak, it has created a personal world that has a certain shape, certain ways of relating, and certain ways of weighing the importance of objects "out there." This is a style of being, an identity theme, that someone else can trace from the adult to earliest childhood. An older metaphysic of subject and object gives way in our time to a sense that one cannot separate subject and object. It is in the very nature of a subject to be always in relation to the world around it through trying out hypotheses and responding to the results. All knowledge is personal knowledge.

These, then, are my six navigational markers or, more accurately, six fundamental hypotheses in psychoanalysis that I have found true and useful:

free association
unconscious dimensions to our language
the image-clusters of childhood stages

a theme-and-variations identity
feedback
potential space

This is, I know, a highly personal synthesis of psychoanalysis. I am not sure any other psychoanalytic critic or any psychoanalyst would say it the same way. Nevertheless, it seems to me these are views widely held by psychoanalytic thinkers. The latest have led to confirming feedback. They seem to me rich with potential. The earliest are thoroughly established. They have withstood the challenges of the nearly-a-century of psychology since Freud.

On an intellectual level, the most strenuous challenge has come from those who claim that psychoanalysis is not "scientific" because it is not testable. As we have seen, this objection is simply not true. Able psychologists, working within a conventional definition of science, have in fact tested psychoanalysis. But notice that this objection does rest on the conventional definition of "scientific" in which observation is independent of the observer.

To me, what is important about psychoanalysis vis-à-vis science is that it challenges and, I think, changes that definition. Psychoanalysis teaches us that all knowledge is knowledge by a person through that person's hypotheses and therefore through their individuality and their culture. In other words, psychoanalysis jibes with recent philosophy of science to say the conclusions of science are not an absolute because the methods of science are not. Science, both its conclusions and its methods, is relative to a particular historical and cultural way of doing science. Psychoanalysis's special contribution is to point out that science is also relative to a particular *individual* style of doing science. Understood this way, psychoanalysis is the science that tells us what other sciences are, because it conceptualizes the individual human beings who do science.

On a practical level, as any American psychoanalyst will tell
you, the biggest challenge to psychoanalysis has come from the ther-
apies that have grown out of psychoanalysis. The challenge is particularly strong in America because of the question of insurance
coverage ("third-party payments"). Insurers, patients, and therapists
alike have recognized that any one of the psychotherapies that have
spun off from psychoanalysis itself may suffice to relieve symptoms,
allay anxiety, or surmount a crisis. No insurance company will pay
for three-to-seven years of five-hour-a-week psychoanalysis if some
months of one-hour-a-week or two-hour-a-week psychotherapy will
cure. Thus another sorry result of our misshapen health policies in
the United States is that clerks in insurance companies look over the
therapist's shoulder. It is they who decide what is or is not
appropriate even in this most private of treatments, psychotherapy.

Psychoanalysis may no longer be the treatment of choice, but
something else: an education, a way of systematically studying
oneself. For that reason it may serve best today as education for
psychiatrists and others planning to be psychotherapists. For them
the full course is absolutely essential. I find it hard to imagine
anyone who intends to practice a "talking cure" who does not need
the special insight into self and others the experience of psychoanalysis gives. I find it equally hard to imagine how someone could
do worthwhile psychoanalytic criticism without what one of the finest
practitioners of the art, Leon Edel, calls a "true inwardness." To do
"literary psychology," he writes, one must understand one's dreams,
one's instincts, one's anxieties, one's personal symbols, the way one
uses fancy to defend oneself within the daily complexities of life.
Above all, one must seek out one's "hidden and anxious *persona*"
(Edel 1981, 465). Only an experience of psychoanalysis can give that
sense of the self. Only a psychoanalytic experience can tell the

literary critic what he or she is bringing to the literature. I do not see how a psychological critic can do without it.

Similarly, I find it hard to believe that "the mind's new science" will not profit from psychoanalytic psychology. Psychoanalysis is the best way we have of conceptualizing individuality or, if you will, subjectivity. I believe there are connections to be made between brain physiology, modern psycholinguistics, artificial intelligence, and cognitive psychology. I have mentioned some writers in these areas in Chapters 3 and 4, and I have tried to make some of these connections myself in *The I*.

In that mode, I can paraphrase Matthew Arnold (and echo something I wrote in 1961, when I first became interested in literature-and-psychoanalysis): the future of psychoanalysis is immense. I believe we are about to relive Freud's vision of psychoanalysis alongside neurology and the biological sciences. I believe we are looking toward a fourth phase of psychoanalysis: psychoanalysis as one contributor to a very much larger science of the mind. I cannot suggest, as with the earlier phases, a fundamental polarity of explanation (conscious vs. unconscious, for example), for such a science seems to me necessarily paradoxical. Psychoanalysis teaches us that all knowledge, including any such science of the mind, will be a personal knowledge. I do not know—perhaps no one yet knows—how to "explain" in such terms.

I feel sure that we shall have to learn, however. If there is one axiom that psychoanalysis gives us, it is that whatever truth we seek "out there," to find it, we shall also have to look within and look back, back into the past and deep within our own minds. That is why this *Guide* is written the way it is and why it reaches the conclusions it does—because all we say and do and know has a personal dimension. That is a psychoanalytic truth that I believe will still hold, no matter how many years from now I were to update this Epilogue.

And now, for something completely different

Personal knowledge. A friend who knows me all too well once said that when I really, really want people to believe what I am saying I make it into a joke. I think that is why I decided not to end this too-serious *Guide* on such a solemn note. Surely we need a final grin and an acknowledgment of the kinds of fun one can have in this field. Not only is there no fee, this is at the expense of psychoanalysis. All work and no play makes psychoanalysts stray.

I'm thinking of the cartoon books like Appignanesi and Zarate's *Freud for Beginners*, a surprisingly accurate introduction whose accuracy doesn't cancel out the wit of the cartoons. Or Ralph Steadman's *Sigmund Freud*, cartoons in the manner of Ronald Searle that mostly sample Freud's theory of jokes. A star in the canon of psychoanalytic joke books is *Freud's Own Cookbook*, edited by James Hillman and Charles Boer (a pair of Jungians!). It features Momovers, Erogenous Scones, Little Hansburgers, Superegonog, and other delights of the oral stage as well as a thoroughly irreverent commentary by *der goldener Sigi* himself. Another star is *Oral Sadism and the Vegetarian Personality*, a series of papers from the *Journal of Polymorphous Perversity* on such topics as "Buddha Meets Kohut," "New Improved Delusions," or "Psychotherapy of the Dead" (Ellenbogen 1986). And now there is a sequel, *The Primal Whimper* (Ellenbogen 1989).

To the Freud fan, hilarious highlights in any collection of parodies of Freud are the opening chapters of D. M. Thomas's otherwise transcendently somber novel, *The White Hotel*. In the opening chapter this imitator *par excellence* brilliantly invents a series of letters to and from Freud and his inner circle in the styles we have come to know and smile at. In the third chapter he creates a whole case history in Freud's own manner. These are not to be missed (and, of course, the novel as a whole is a stunning performance).

Much more of a pop novel is Judith Rossner's *August* (1983), yet for all that it gives an accurate picture of a New York psychoanalysis today. The analyst, whose own life is something of a shambles, is trying to help a beautiful but troubled Barnard freshman. August is the month in which analysts traditionally take their vacations, and Rossner's novel makes a fascinating study of separation anxiety.

Paul Buttonwieser's *Free Association* (1981) takes us to the very beach in Wellfleet, Cape Cod (once the retreat of Edmund Wilson and Mary McCarthy), where nowadays East Coast analysts go in August. (It is said to be the only beach in America where, if you lie down to sunbathe and strike up a conversation with a stranger, you will receive a bill the next day.) Buttonwieser paints a delightfully satiric (not satyric!) picture of the New York psychoanalytic scene, both on and off vacation. The novel details the experiences of a pathetically sex-starved psychoanalytic candidate. He answers an ad in the *Village Voice*: "SJF, 27, into art, tennis, politics, seeks SM 25-35 . . . let come what may!" What comes is that the SJF turns out to be one of his patients.

Samuel Shem's *Fine* (1985) uses all the puns that that title, the analyst-hero's name, makes possible. He looks with jaundiced eye at the Boston psychoanalytic scene and comes out in favor of life with a capital L instead of analysis with a capital A.

Buttonwieser's version of the New York Psychoanalytic Institute appears in more serious form in Janet Malcolm's well-known essay, *Psychoanalysis: The Impossible Profession* (1981), a painfully funny journalistic study of psychoanalysis as an institution, at least in one of most orthodox American incarnations. (For the

French version of that institution, see Sherry Turkle's *Psychoanalytic Politics*, and for the English, see Phyllis Grosskurth's *Melanie Klein*, both more scholarly accounts.) Another of Janet Malcolm's journalistic studies of psychoanalysis is also not to be missed. Her *In the Freud Archives* is like an old movie: *Abbott and Costello Meet Frankenstein*. Here, two obsessionals meet a psychopath. Malcolm tells the story of Jeffrey Masson's appointment by Kurt Eissler as Secretary of the Freud Archives, followed by his supposed discovery of the "real" reason Freud rejected his hypothesis that the cause of hysteria was actual seductions, followed by Masson's being fired by Eissler and Anna Freud, followed by lawsuits, books, and articles by Masson. An unpleasant story that has its comic moments.

The core psychoanalytic novel is Italo Svevo's classic account of his hero's efforts to quit smoking through psychoanalysis: *Confessions of Zeno*. Of the more recent psychoanalytic novels I know, the farthest out is surely Barry N. Malzberg's sci-fi novel, *The Re-Making of Sigmund Freud* (1985) in which a reconstructed twenty-fourth century Freud in a space suit tries to analyze a crazed Venusian colonist and cure the hysterical pains of a Vegan alien. There are dozens more collected and studied by Jeffrey Berman (1985). And of course there are plays: Saul Bellow's *The Last Analysis* and even the well-known musical, Kurt Weill's *Lady in the Dark*.

To say nothing of the movies. The most authentic is G. W. Pabst's *Secrets of a Soul* (*Geheimnisse einer Seele* [1926]). Freud refused even to see Sam Goldwyn when that archetypal Hollywood producer proposed to consult "the greatest love expert in the world." Likewise, when the huge German production company UFA asked Freud to act as technical adviser to Pabst's film, he again refused. Karl Abraham and Hanns Sachs, however, did agree to do it, and the movie does depict (in cinematic language!) classical, first-phase psychoanalysis. A disturbed man meets a stranger in a bar, and they begin a conversation. Much is made of keys, locks, umbrellas, spikes, and other symbols, which the stranger proudly decodes and then proclaims, "*I* am a psychoanalyst." Unintentionally funny, audiences laugh at this quaint version of psychoanalysis, but it is the nearest thing we have to a film Freud himself might have okayed. But then Freud didn't like the movies (except for Charlie Chaplin).

A more famous version is John Huston's *Freud* (1961), starring Montgomery Clift in the title role. Clift's facial muscles had been badly cut in an automobile accident, and he was thereby able to maintain a stolid "analytic neutrality" even in this cinematic, but otherwise fairly preposterous film. When it was re-released, a subtitle was added that gives something of the flavor: it became *Freud: The Secret Passion*. In the same vein, Huston's voice-over introduced the movie as "the story of Freud's descent into a region almost as black as hell itself—man's unconscious—and how he let in the light." What would Freud have said to these almost Christ-like terms?

To make Freud's years of painful self-analysis and discovery into a movie, Huston collapsed it all into a single night. He has Sigmund sitting up till daybreak excitedly telling Martha the method of free association, the cause and cure of neuroses, the oedipus complex, the reason we laugh at jokes, the secret of dreams, and on and on. Finally, he throws the curtains open to light and the new dawn. That is called *symbolism*.

Even more remarkable than the picture itself was what went on before the picture. Huston decided that only one man in the world could write a movie about Freud—Jean-Paul Sartre. In addition, Huston and Sartre wanted Marilyn Monroe for the role of Frau Cäcilie (the composite patient who is the heroine). Monroe's analyst objected, saying Anna Freud would oppose such a plan. Sartre was perhaps enough all by himself. He created the startling image of a bored Freud massaging the thighs and bottom of Cäcilie lying on her stomach clad only in her underwear and black stockings. This perhaps tells us more about Sartre than Freud. Ultimately, Sartre's script had to be rejected as hopelessly too long. It would have made a seven-hour movie. "One could make a movie four hours long if it is about *Ben Hur*," Sartre later sneered, "but the public in Texas will not stand for four hours of complexes." Huston turned to a couple of Hollywood regulars for his final script.

Huston was not the only major director to deal with psychoanalysis and psychiatry. There are Ingmar Bergman's rich, if somber, studies. There is the ending to Hitchcock's *Psycho* (1960), where Dr. Richmond explains it all. Apparently, Hitchcock himself meant it seriously. Others (myself, for example) think it parody. Then there is Ingrid Bergman's lovesick cure of Gregory Peck in *Spellbound* (1945). Again Hitchcock seems to think he has portrayed psychoanalysts realistically. Again it seems more like parody--except for the senior training analyst played by the *gemütlich* Michael Chekhov (the playwright's nephew).

The one moviemaker for whom psychoanalysis has proved an endless gold mine is, of course, Woody Allen. As he says in *Hannah and her Sisters* (1986): "I was in analysis for years. Nothing happened. My analyst got so frustrated, the poor guy, that he put in a salad bar." Allen seems to be making back both the fees he paid and whatever positive transference he had. In *Stardust Memories* (1980), he fantasies a huge hairy monster that represents "Sidney Finkelstein's hostility." Surrounded by the dead bodies of all the people Sidney hates, the monster is pursued by police and hunting dogs, when a man in a dark raincoat steps toward the monster and calls out, "Please, uh, we don't want to hurt you. We . . . we want to reason with you. I'm a psychoanalyst. This is my pipe." Sometimes a pipe is only a pipe.

If only the Hollywood types drawn to psychoanalysis were as knowledgeable as Woody Allen. Krin and Glen O. Gabbard in their definitive survey (on which I am drawing extensively and gratefully) list some 271, count 'em, 271 movies, mostly Hollywood, that use psychiatry as a large or small part. Their list begins auspiciously with the immortal *Dr. Dippy's Sanitarium* in 1906 and runs to *Down and Out in Beverly Hills* eighty years later.

There are some well-known and quite wonderful movies among the 271 that feature psychoanalysts or psychiatrists. Some treat psychiatry reverently: *David and Lisa* (1962) or *Ordinary People* (1980). Slightly less reverent are Woody Allen's movies: *Annie Hall* (1977) or *Interiors* (1978) or *Zelig* (1983) where the Human Chameleon joins the Freud circle. Still less reverent are the great screwball comedies, which often featured a buffoon psychiatrist: Howard Hawks's *Bringing Up Baby* (1938) or *His Girl Friday* (1940) or, in that same year, Garson Kanin's *My Favorite Wife*. Many of the movies' classics have psychiatric episodes. There is a psychiatrist in Tod Browning's wonderful *Dracula* (1931) who does not believe in vampires, just as there is a psychiatrist in *The Terminator* (1984) who does not believe in Arnold Schwarzenegger. Let us not forget that there's a psychiatrist in *Willy Wonka and the Chocolate Factory* (1971), or one of my favorites, *Three Nuts in Search of a Bolt* (1964).

In those 271 movies, a truly astonishing range of actors have played psychiatrists: Boris Karloff, Bela Lugosi, Vincent Price, and Peter Sellers—you'd expect them, of course, but what about Fred Astaire, Charles Boyer, and Hedy Lamarr? And let us not forget the professor of psychology played by Ronald Reagan in *Bedtime for Bonzo* (1951). He teaches a chimpanzee morality in that movie, foreshadowing his later career. Alan Arkin played Freud in *The Seven Percent Solution* (1976), a Freud who is called in, not for psychiatry, but to help Sherlock Holmes cure his cocaine habit.

Nevertheless, Arkin plays a particularly appealing Freud, one who defeats and humiliates a pompous Austro-Hungarian anti-semite in a tennis match by psyching out his backhand.

Among the many actors who have played patients and analysands, surely the most unlikely is Elvis Presley in *Wild in the Country* (1961). In this script by no less than Clifford Odets, Hope Lange plays Elvis Presley's psychiatrist. Although Presley dismisses her statements about "transference" as "book talk," she cures him of whatever and sends him off to college where, under the tutelage of a likable English professor, he will grow up to be a William Faulkner, all because he had "professional help."

From 1906 to 1986, we see Hollywood develop the standard clichés of movie psychiatry. Patients get cured when, in one astonishing moment, they remember some equally dramatic moment from childhood. Psychiatrists are all Viennese. Female psychiatrists are either hopelessly desexed or rescued from their grotesque profession by the love of a good man that takes them into marriage and motherhood.

The Gabbards trace a pattern in these 271 movies. At first, Hollywood treats psychoanalysis or psychiatry as mysterious and foreign. The psychiatrist is stereotyped as a Viennese wearing a tailcoat and a pince-nez, and he speaks with some kind of a Cherman accent. Sometimes he is a quack, and always he is wrong or ridiculous. Gradually, however, Hollywood begins to treat the psychiatrist as having more and more power, sometimes of a dangerous kind. Then, note the Gabbards, 1957-1963 marks a kind of golden period when psychiatry is reverenced and idealized, and we are shown sensitive, intelligent, American psychiatrists. After that, come the years of "flower power" or Nixon-Reagan conservatism. Psychiatry is treated irreverently, for two opposite reasons. Flower power sees it as dangerously repressive. Conservatives see it as dangerously opening up possibilities. In these movies the good, omniscient psychiatrist shades over into the powerful misguider, the caring psychiatrist to the lecherous, the strong to the murderous, and so on.

One of the most startling of these recent antipsychiatry movies is Marshall Brickman's 1983 film *Lovesick*, in which from time to time, Alec Guiness as the spirit of Freud appears to the lovesick psychoanalyst to offer cold comfort. "Psychoanalysis is an interesting method," he says. "I never intended it to become an industry." Oh?

Then there is the BBC television series, *Freud*. Done in glowing colors and lush décor by actors who remarkably resemble the photos of those early days, it looks the most authentic and "Viennese" of the filmed accounts. That is unfortunate, for its script elevates gossip to the status of history: Freud's supposed homosexual longings for his early confidant Fliess; Freud's supposed affair with his wife's sister Minna. Much, naturally, is made of Freud's infatuation with cocaine, indeed, to the point where it rather overshadows his later discovery of psychoanalysis. (The French speak of *cet inconscience qui sniffait trop*.)

Cartoons, novels, movies, television—these are only a few of the marvels that await the assiduous researcher, aided, of course, by a reader's guide like this. Imagine, for example, being able actually to sit down and play the popular song of 1925 that John Burnham (1978) refers to: "Don't Tell Me What You Dreamed Last Night, For I've Been Reading Freud." A moment like that could repay a lifetime of reading psychoanalysis. A moment like that, especially at its merriest, will be a truly personal knowledge.

6

Research Aids

Prepared with the help of William McPheron (Stanford University Libraries)

I HAVE ORGANIZED this list of research aids as follows:

Guides to the Literature
Dictionaries
Handbooks and Encyclopedias
Bibliographies, Indexes, and Abstracts
Directories
Other Useful Tools

I have marked with a pound sign (#) those items that seem to me particularly relevant to psychoanalytic research (as opposed, say, to bibliographies that cover all of psychology). I have marked with a square bullet (■) those items that are particularly relevant *and* that can be searched on-line through such information services as DIALOG, BRS, INFOQUEST, or EASYLINK.

GUIDES TO THE LITERATURE

Bell, James Edward. *A Guide to Library Research in Psychology.* Dubuque IA: W. C. Brown, 1971.

Freides, Thelma. *Literature and Bibliography of the Social Sciences.* Los Angeles: Melville Publishing Co., 1973.

\# Grimaud, Michel. "Recent Trends in Psychoanalysis: A Survey, with Emphasis on Psychological Criticism in English Literature and Related Areas [in the Social Sciences]." *Sub-Stance* 13 (1976): 136-162.

\# Grimaud, Michel. "Part Three: A Reader's Guide to Psychoanalysis. An Overview of Psychoanalytic Theory and the Psychoanalytic Approach in Literary Theory and Practice, with Emphasis on French Studies." William J. Berg, Michel Grimaud, and George Moskos. *Saint/Oedipus: Psychocritical Approaches to Flaubert's Art.* Ithaca and London: Cornell University Press, 1982.

> The two extremely useful texts by Grimaud list and partially annotate English and French materials in such categories as: Reference Tools; Introductions to Psychoanalysis; Psychoanalytic Journals; Classic Papers; Methodology; and various specific topics (Dreams; Readers; Feminism; Homosexuality; Myth; etc.) as well as literary theory and criticism. The 1976 text includes an unusual "Introductory Reading List."

Grimaud, Michel. "Poetics from Psychoanalysis to Cognitive
Psychology." *Poetics* 13 (1984): 325-345.

As much essay as survey, this article notes that literary
critics rely primarily on psychologies of emotion and
motivation in their earliest versions (e.g., Freud, Jung, or
Horney). Grimaud summarizes recent psychoanalysis
(ego psychology, object-relations theory, self psychology,
Lacan) and relates the psychoanalytic account of cognitive and psychosexual developmental stages to contemporary cognitive psychology. He urges a synthesis of
modern psychoanalysis and cognitive psychology and
shows how some American and German "poeticians"
are building it.

Li, Tze-chung. *Social Science Reference Sources: A Practical
Guide.* Westport CT: Greenwood Press, 1980.

*Resources for the Psychoanalyst: A Select Guide to Published
Material and Information Sources for the 31st Congress of the
International Psycho-Analytical Association, July 29-August 3,
1979, New York City.* Ed. Phyllis Rubinton, Lee Mackler,
Liselotte Bendix Stern, and Katharine B. Wolpe. New York:
[International Universities Press], 1979.

This 22-page pamphlet lists: Libraries and Bibliographic
Reference Services; Libraries in the New York Area;
Psychoanalytic Libraries outside the New York Area;
Sources for Freud and Historic Material; Indexes and
Abstracts; Periodicals (English, French, German,
Hungarian, Italian, Japanese, Portuguese, and Spanish);
Series [of annual volumes]; Bookstores and Book Deal-

ers (New York Area); and Addresses of Publishers. The list of special collections would be of particular interest to anyone doing historical research. It was especially prepared for the 1979 IPA meeting and has, unfortunately, not been reprinted or updated.

\# Schwartz, Murray M., and David Willbern. "Literature and Psychology." *Interrelations of Literature*. Ed. Jean-Pierre Barricelli and Joseph Gibaldi. New York: Modern Language Association of America, 1982. 205-224.

This essay briefly and expertly surveys the field and its history, concluding with a selective bibliography of dictionaries, bibliographies, theoretical texts, anthologies of criticism, books and articles in practical criticism, and periodicals receptive to this approach.

White, Carl M. *Sources of Information in the Social Sciences*. 2d ed. Chicago: American Library Association, 1973.

DICTIONARIES

\# Campbell, Robert Jean, ed. *Psychiatric Dictionary*. 5th ed. New York: Oxford University Press, 1981.

More narrowly focused than English (see next page) and intended principally for professional use, this dictionary has long been considered authoritative in the field. Definitions are expansive, with care taken to trace the historical evolution or ideological context of terms. All schools of psychiatry are represented, with the treatment of psychoanalysis itself quite thorough. This is an update of a 1970 edition by Leland E. Hinsie and Robert Jean Campbell.

Drever, James. Rev. Harvey Wallerstein. *A Dictionary of Psychology*. Baltimore MD: Penguin Books, 1975.

English, Horace Bidwell, and Ava C. English. *A Comprehensive Dictionary of Psychological and Psychoanalytical Terms*. New York: David MacKay, 1958.

Long a standard reference source, this dictionary, though now dated, is unusually exhaustive in its coverage of the specialized terminology in the fields of both psychology and psychoanalysis. Definitions are concise, with plentiful cross references but no bibliographical references to other sources.

Fodor, Nandor, and Frank Gaynor, eds. *Freud: Dictionary of Psychoanalysis*. New York: Philosophical Library, 1958.

The title is something of a misnomer. This is a collection of relevant quotations from Freud under alphabetical headings. It is handy for locating useful statements from Freud on topics where the alphabetical index to the *Standard Edition* would yield an impossibly large number of references. It is, however, based on the older translations of Freud, and it is not indexed by page, but one could use the Freud *Concordance* to locate quotations found in this work in the *Standard Edition*.

\# Laplanche, J., and Pontalis, J. B. *The Language of Psychoanalysis*. New York: Norton, 1973.

Focusing exclusively on the concepts of psychoanalysis proper, this dictionary provides an unusually thorough treatment of the terms it includes. Emphasis is on Freud, with explanatory definitions tracing concepts from their origins in his work. All entries conclude with citations of relevant passages in Freud or the writings of his followers. This is an excellent tool for obtaining a detailed introduction to the basic ideas of psychoanalysis in its contemporary French version. It lacks, however, terms useful in psychoanalysis as a whole (such as "character").

\# Moore, Burness E., and Bernard D. Fine, eds. *A Glossary of Psychoanalytic Terms and Concepts.* New York: American Psychoanalytic Association, 1967.

This is a definitive glossary of terms with extensive cross-referencing and a time-saving list of terms *not* defined. The definitions do not refer to other texts, but the book includes a basic bibliography which would serve as an introductory reading list. All this, however, comes from the point of view of American ego-psychology (second-phase psychoanalysis) and may seem narrow in the 1990s.

\# Rycroft, Charles. *A Critical Dictionary of Psychoanalysis.* Totowa NJ: Littlefield, Adams, 1973.

Emphasizing but not confined to Freudian psychoanalysis, this highly readable dictionary provides not only concise definitions of technical terms but also accounts of their origins and their connections with other con-

cepts in the field. Thorough cross references place individual terms in the total framework of psychoanalytic
theory, while references within the entries to the
volume's bibliography point to fuller discussions.
Unfortunately, as of 1989, this excellent work is out of
print.

Stone, Evelyn M., comp. and ed. *American Psychiatric Glossary*.
6th ed. Washington DC: American Psychiatric Press, 1988.

Published by the American Psychiatric Association as
being "of interest to the general public," this is fairly
elementary. It covers all kinds of psychiatric terms and
its definitions do incorporate the DSM-III. It also gives
tables of abused drugs, drugs used in psychiatry,
neurological deficits, psychological tests, research terms,
and schools of psychiatry. And it contains a bibliography. This is a revised edition of the American
Psychiatric Association's 1981 psychiatric glossary, the
5th edition, which was more professionally oriented (see
Campbell).

Wolman, Benjamin B. *Dictionary of Behavioral Science*. New
York: Van Nostrand Reinhold Co., 1973.

HANDBOOKS AND ENCYCLOPEDIAS

No one of this group of references treats all topics equally well
or, indeed, all topics. All are quite condensed. Researching this
diverse and rapidly changing field, you should consult as many as
possible and especially the most recent available.

American Handbook of Psychiatry. 2d ed. Ed. Silvano Arieti.
New York: Basic Books, 1974-1976.

This multivolume tool provides a thorough and scholarly
survey of the topics and approaches of contemporary
psychiatry. Intended as a source of condensed but
authoritative information for professionals in the field,
the set focuses its volumes on different areas of the subject. For example, Vol. 1 concentrates on the historical
foundations of psychiatry, including separate accounts of
all major schools, while Vol. 6 emphasizes new
developments. Each volume has its own subject index to
allow a more precise approach to topics.

Comprehensive Textbook of Psychiatry IV. Ed. Harold I. Kaplan
and Benjamin J. Sadock. 4th ed. 2 volumes. Baltimore MD :
Williams & Wilkins, 1985.
Kaplan, Harold I. *Modern Synopsis of Comprehensive Textbook
of Psychiatry IV.* 4th ed. Baltimore MD: Williams & Wilkins,
1985.

\# Corsini, Raymond J., ed. *Encyclopedia of Psychology.* 4 volumes.
New York: Wiley-Interscience, 1984.

This is probably the best overall of the encyclopedias (by
virtue of its size if nothing else). It covers topics
throughout psychology, psychoanalysis, and psychiatry in
considerable depth. The whole fourth volume consists
of bibliography and thorough indexes. It is unusual in
offering sketches of psychology in various nations. The
entry on literature and psychology (by J. Bieri) is quite
good.

Corsini, Raymond J., ed. *Concise Encyclopedia of Psychology.*
New York : Wiley-Interscience, 1987.

The *Concise* contains some 55% of the 4-volume version. Biographies are particularly reduced, but all the
old entries are retained and updated and some new ones
added (notably "Artificial Intelligence" by Herbert A.
Simon).

Encyclopedia of Clinical Assessment. San Francisco: Jossey-
Bass, 1980. 2 volumes.

Encyclopedia of Mental Health. New York: Franklin Watts,
1963. 6 volumes.

Eysenck, H. J. *Handbook of Abnormal Psychology.* 2d ed. San
Diego CA: Robert R. Knapp, 1973.

Eysenck, H. J., W. Arnold, and R. Meili, eds. *Encyclopedia of
Psychology.* New York: Herder and Herder, 1972.

Goldenson, Robert M., ed. *The Encyclopedia of Human Behavior: Psychology, Psychiatry, and Mental Health.* Garden City NY:
Doubleday, 1970.

The two preceding encyclopedias are designed principally for the nonprofessional reader. They cover the
broad gamut of psychological topics in an abbreviated
but reliable manner. Less technical than other
encyclopedias listed here, they can be useful for providing introductory treatments of basic concepts and terms.

Hales, Robert E., and Stuart C. Yudofsky, eds. *The American Psychiatric Press Textbook of Neuropsychiatry*. 1st ed. Washington DC: American Psychiatric Press, 1988.

\# Hampden-Turner, Charles. *Maps of the Mind*. New York: Macmillan, 1981.

This popularization provides one- and two-page introductions to sixty psychological, psychoanalytic, and philosophical thinkers about the mind, including instructive diagrams and brief bibliographies. It is elementary but fun.

\# Harré, Rom, and Roger Lamb. *The Encyclopedic Dictionary of Psychology*. Cambridge MA: MIT Press, 1983.

This dictionary-encyclopedia is slanted toward "the mind's new science" (reflecting its British origins and M.I.T. publishers). Eclectic, it accents cognitive psychology, psycholinguistics, and neurophysiology. It expands from there into developmental psychology, social and personality psychology, and the psychology of emotions. It addresses philosophical issues (e.g., the mind-body problem, the problem of other minds). And it includes "fringe psychologies" (e.g., astrology, primal scream, Rosicrucians, Rolfing). It includes psychiatric, psychoanalytic, psycholinguistic, as well as psychological terms. There is an excellent index and glossary. J. Forrester's entries on Lacan, though succinct, are most helpful.

Nicholi, Armand M., Jr., ed. *The New Harvard Guide to Psychiatry.* Cambridge MA: Harvard Univ. Press, 1988.

An introduction to the principal branches and topics of contemporary psychiatry, this work focuses on the technically accurate presentation of core information. Each chapter covers a different topic and acts both as a guide to central concepts and to basic literature in the field. An excellent index provides access to discussions of both subjects and ideas of individual theorists. The 1988 "new" edition responds to various changes between 1978 and 1985: vastly improved brain scanning methods, advances in the genetics of mental illness; increases in eating disorders, adolescent suicide, psychoactive drug use, and the AIDS epidemic. There are chapters on the DSM-III-R.

Like the *American Psychiatric* (see Talbott), this encyclopedia covers all of psychiatry in many chapters by many authors. The *New Harvard*, however, is more accessible to the non-medical reader and written with a notable devotion to style. Most authors are from the Harvard Medical School (whose departments of psychiatry include some 1800 persons!), and they express the strong psychoanalytic tradition of that institution.

Chapter 9 by W. W. Meisser provides an excellent introduction to dynamic personality theories: Freud's, Adler's, Jung's, M. Klein's, Reich's, Horney's, Sullivan's, Kohut's, Kernberg's and others. Meissner also covers psychological methods with personality like information theory or factor analysis.

International Encyclopedia of the Social Sciences. New York: Macmillan, 1968. 17 volumes.

International Encyclopedia of Psychiatry, Psychology, Psychoanalysis and Neurology. Ed. Benjamin B. Wolman. New York: Aesculapius Publishers, 1977.

This is regarded as one of the most comprehensive and authoritative sources in the field. Covering a broad range of topics from a variety of disciplines, the work is distinguished by its lengthy and detailed articles, almost all of which are supported by useful bibliographies.

Neel, Ann. *Theories of Psychology: A Handbook.* Rev. ed. New York: Wiley, 1977.

This tool is designed to provide concise accounts of the various schools of psychological thought. Major figures and topics are accorded separate chapters, buttressed by lengthy bibliographies. The volume serves especially well as an overview of the competing explanatory and therapeutic models of twentieth-century psychology.

\# *The Oxford Companion to the Mind.* Ed. Richard L. Gregory with O. I. Zangwill. New York: Oxford UP, 1987.

This may be the best of these encyclopedias for the lay person. Unfortunately it is very uneven in quality, and it has eccentricities, like entries on Hands, Lying, or Diver Performance. Although it has entries on non-Western psychologies, it omits anthropology entirely. It is, however, particularly strong on cognitive and perceptual psychology, neuroscience, brain anatomy, and

philosophical issues. It is fairly good on psychiatric and
psychoanalytic categories. If warily read, it can be very
useful.

Talbott, John A., Robert E. Hales, and Stuart C. Yudofsky, eds.
The American Psychiatric Press Textbook of Psychiatry. 1st ed.
Washington DC: American Psychiatric Press, 1988.

Quite technical, written for M.D.s and oriented toward
diagnosis and therapy, this encylopedia surveys all of
psychiatry in many chapters by many authors. It rests on
the principle of close association between neurologic
conditions (e.g., stroke) and conditions associated with
the behavioral sciences (e.g., substance abuse). It does,
however, cover topics of interest in literature-and-
psychology (such as suicide or psychiatry and culture).
Appendices include diagnostic criteria from the DSM-
III-R and some definitions from E. M. Stone's *American
Psychiatric Glossary*. S. S. Marmer's chapter on theories
of the mind by Freud, M. Klein, Fairbairn, Bowlby,
Kohut, Kernberg, et al., is strongly recommended.

BIBLIOGRAPHIES, INDEXES, AND ABSTRACTS

American Behavioral Scientist. *The ABS Guide to Recent Publications in the Social and Behavioral Sciences*. New York: Sage
Publications, 1965. Supplements. New York: Sage Publications,
1966- .

Bleich, David, Eugene R. Kintgen, Bruce Smith, and Sandor J.
Vargyai. "The Psychological Study of Language and Literature:

A Selected and Annotated Bibliography." *Style* 12 (1978): 113-210.

"This list represents what the compilers consider to be some of the more significant research initiatives in the attempt to understand language and literature as aspects of human psychology." The principle of selection, however, is not given. The list is usefully organized into 17 sections based on psycholinguistic and reader-response categories. Although a great deal has happened in this field since 1978, this resource will get one started with reader-response and psycholinguistic materials. It is less helpful with psychoanalytic studies.

Catalog of Selected Documents in Psychology. Washington: American Psychological Association, vol. 1- , 1971- .

Documents are on microfiche.

- *Chicago Psychoanalytic Literature Index, 1920-1970*. Chicago: CPL Publishing, 1978.

    Covering both articles and books but focusing principally on English language materials, this index represents the catalog of the Chicago Institute for Psychoanalysis. The first volume is arranged by authors; the other two are highly specific subject indexes. This is a useful complement to the coverage and treatment furnished by Grinstein (see below). It can be searched on-line by telephoning the Chicago Psychoanalytic Institute.

- *Chicago Psychoanalytic Literature Index, 1975*. Chicago: Institute for Psychoanalysis, 1976.

Beginning with books and articles published in 1975, these annual volumes update the coverage of the basic *CPL Index* and provide reasonably current treatment of psychoanalytic writings generally. Materials dealing explicitly with literary topics can be located under broad headings (e.g., "Literature," "Science Fiction"). Individual authors and works may be searched under the general rubric, Biography-Criticism.

Child Development Abstracts and Bibliography. Washington DC: National Research Council, vol. 1- , 1927- .

\# Clark, Michael, comp. *Jacques Lacan: An Annotated Bibliography.* 2 volumes. Garland Reference Library of the Humanities. Vol. 526. New York and London: Garland Publishing, 1988.

Communications/Research/Machines, Inc. *Psychosources: A Psychology Resource Catalog.* New York: Bantam Books, 1973.

■ *Dissertation Abstracts International.* Ann Arbor MI: University Microfilms, vol. 12- , 1952- .

■ *Excerpta Medica: Section 8, Neurology and Psychiatry.* v. 1, no. 1, Jan. 1948—v. 18, no. 12, Dec. 1965. Amsterdam and New York: Excerpta Medica Foundation. Continued in parts by: *Excerpta Medica: Section 8A, Neurology and neurosurgery* v. 19- , 1966- and: *Excerpta Medica, Section 8B, Psychiatry* v. 19-21, 1966-68, and *Excerpta Medica, Section 32, Psychiatry,* v. 22- , no. 1, Jan. 1969- .

A monthly selective abstracting service covering world medical journals. Includes section on psychoanalysis and separate author and subject indexes, cumulated semiannually. Non-English-language literature is covered well. It can be searched on-line in DIALOG and BRS.

Grinstein, Alexander. *The Index of Psychoanalytic Writings*. New York: International Universities Press, 1956-1975. 14 volumes.

This is one of the foremost bibliographic sources for psychoanalytic literature generally. Grinstein's *Index* revises and updates Rickman's *Index Psychoanalyticus* (see next page). It covers articles, books, and reviews published from 1900-1969. This coverage is provided in three sections (Vols. 1-5: 1900-1952; Vols. 6-9: 1953-1959; Vols. 10-14: 1960-1969), each of which is arranged alphabetically by authors' names, with an excellent subject index. These index volumes (Vols. 5, 9, 14) furnish access by detailed concept as well as broad topic. The entries under both "Literary" and "Literature" are extensive.

Hart, Henry Harper. *Conceptual Index to Psychoanalytic Technique and Training*. (n.p.): North River Press, 1972. 5 volumes.

Harvard University. *The Harvard List of Books in Psychology*. 4th ed. Cambridge, Massachusetts: Harvard Press, 1971.

■ *Index Medicus*. Bethesda, Maryland: National Library of Medicine, 1960- .

■ *Cumulated Index Medicus*. Bethesda, Maryland: National
Library of Medicine, 1960.

> This comprehensive index to the world's medical litera-
> ture covers psychiatry and psychoanalysis as well as
> selected areas of psychology. Issued monthly, the *Index*
> is gathered annually into its cumulated format. The sub-
> ject section is very detailed and treatment is quite cur-
> rent. Though its emphasis is on the physiological
> aspects of medicine, the *Index Medicus* does serve as a
> useful supplementary source for psychoanalysis and psy-
> chology. Its contents can also be searched on-line, often
> for free.

Index Psychoanalyticus. 1893-1926. Compiled by John Rickman.
London: Hogarth Press, 1928 (The International Psycho-
Analytical Library #14).

> An alphabetically arranged author index of papers on
> psychoanalysis. Editorial notes in English, French, and
> German. Alternate publications and translations are
> listed.

IPSA Abstracts and Bibliography in Literature and Psychology.
Published by the Institute for Psychological Study of the Arts,
4008 Turlington Hall, University of Florida, Gainesville, Florida
32611. Distributed to members of the Psychological Approaches
Division, Modern Language Association and others. $5.00 con-
tribution requested. v. 1- , 1986- .

> Published in April or May, this booklet lists books and
> articles in the field of literature-and-psychology and, to

some extent, psychoanalysis in general that have been
published in the preceding year. It also provides
abstracts of articles that have been accepted for publication but not yet published. The aim is to circulate
ideas and information faster than the ordinary
humanities bibliographies do.

\# JOURLIT and BOOKREV. 1920-1986. Diskettes available,
respectively, from Stanley Goodman, M.D., 3021 Telegraph Ave.,
Berkeley CA 94705 ($25) and Vann Spruiell, M.D., 1305
Antonine St., New Orleans LA 70115 ($25).

This is a nonprofit cottage industry of some psychoanalysts who have entered on IBM-format diskettes the
author, title, volume, page, and date of all the journal
articles (JOURLIT) and book reviews (BOOKREV) in
the *Journal of the American Psychoanalytic Association*,
Psychoanalytic Quarterly, *International Journal* and *International Review of Psycho-Analysis*, and *Psychoanalytic
Study of the Child* (no book reviews). With a personal
computer, the diskettes can be searched either crudely,
by means of a word processor, or Booleanly by PC-
FILE+ (a "shareware" database program that exists in
various versions). Using PC-FILE+, one can also keep
the database up to date on one's own. A printout of just
the JOURLIT database is also available: see below, *Title
Key Word and Author Index*.

\# Kiell, Norman. *Psychoanalysis, Psychology, and Literature: A
Bibliography*. 2d ed. Metuchen NJ: Scarecrow, 1982.

This is *the* index for literature-and-psychology. It
focuses exclusively on materials dealing with literary
works from a specifically psychological or psychoanalytic
perspective. Both books and periodical articles are
included, with coverage extending to approximately
1980. The first volume is arranged by broad topics (e.g.,
"Fiction," "Poetry," "Drama"). The second volume
serves as an index, with separate listings for writers,
works, and subjects discussed. If anything, Kiell tends to
over-include, so this is the bibliography to start with,
then pare down.

\# Meurs, Jos van, with John Kidd. *Jungian Literary Criticism, 1920-
1980: An Annotated, Critical Bibliography of Works in English
(with a Selection of Titles after 1980).* Metuchen, NJ: Scarecrow
Press, 1988.

This bibliography's 900 entries include books, articles,
and all doctoral dissertations that interpret literature by
means of a "substantial" use of the analytic psychology
of Jung or his disciples such as Joseph Campbell, Erich
Neumann, or James Hillman. All entries are annotated,
and important titles have lengthy summaries and
extensive critical evaluations. In both text and index the
author indicates the studies he regards as most important. An opening essay reviews developments and
achievements in Jungian criticism over the period.

\# Natoli, Joseph, and Frederik L. Rusch, comps. *Psychocriticism:
An Annotated Bibliography*. Bibliographies and Indexes in World
Literature, Number 1. Westport CT and London: Greenwood P,
1984.

Less inclusive than Kiell, *Psychocriticism* focuses more tightly on works applying a particular psychological approach (psychoanalytic but also Jungian, Reichian, etc.). It is particularly helpful in providing abstracts of the items. Both the Preface and Introductory Essay are useful overviews, respectively, of other bibliographies and psychological approaches to literature generally.

\# Pfeiffer, Joachim, comp. *Literaturepsychologie 1945-1987: Eine Systematische und Annotierte Bibliographie.* Würzburg: König-sheim und Neumann, 1989.

Unavailable to me at the time this *Guide* went to press, I assume this bibliography will prove strong on Continental materials in literature-and-psychology. Note that it is annotated.

■ *Psychological Abstracts.* Arlington VA: American Psychological Association, vol. 1- , 1927- .

Published monthly and covering books, articles, and other relevant documents, this tool provides the most thorough and current coverage available of psychological literature. Arrangement is by broad topic, e.g. "Psychometrics," "Developmental Psychology," with brief author and subject indexes in monthly issues and highly detailed ones for each complete volume. Although emphasis is on experimental and clinical psychology, the coverage is sufficiently broad to include numerous references to literary studies from both psychological and psychoanalytic points of view. Such general headings as "Literature," "Prose," and "Poetry"

must be used to identify these. Cumulative subject and
author indexes are available to simplify searching in
volumes published prior to 1978. Materials listed since
1967 can also be searched on-line in the database
PSYCINFO (available in DIALOG or CompuServe) or
searched off-line by means of the PsycLIT CD-ROM.

Psychological Index. Princeton NJ: Psychological Review Co.,
vol. 1-42, 1894-1935.

PsycSCAN: PSYCHOANALYSIS. Arlington VA: American Psy-
chological Association, vol. 1- , 1987- .

A biannual publication (June and December) by Division 39 of the American Psychological Association,
PsycSCAN: PSYCHOANALYSIS abstracts all recent
articles in a very large list of psychoanalytic journals,
annually selected by the editors. Included are foreign
journals (abstracted in English) and Jungian, Adlerian,
Horneyan, etc., articles. Abstracts are presented
alphabetically by journal and then by page number
within the journal. There is, unfortunately, no index, but
each abstract provides index terms (the rather broad
terms of the *Thesaurus of Psychological Index Terms*),
and one can search these on-line in PSYCINFO or by
hand in *Psychological Abstracts*. This is a new and most
important addition to the aids for psychoanalytic
research, highly valuable for keeping *au courant*.

Rothenberg, Albert, and Bette Greenberg, comps. *The Index of
Scientific Writings on Creativity*. New York: Archon. Volume 1:

Creative Men and Women, 1974. Volume 2: *General, 1566-1974*, 1976.

> The first volume contains articles on creative people in literature, art, music, and dance. The second deals with creativity in general. Unfortunately, the "Scientific" in the title means that the compilers have not included the many articles in this field in literary, philosophical, or other humanistic or social science journals. The bibliography is not annotated.

Social Sciences Index. New York: H. W. Wilson Co., vol. 1- , 1974- .

\# *Title Key Word and Author Index to Psychoanalytic Journals: 1920-1986*. Ed. Paul W. Mosher, M.D. New York: American Psychoanalytic Association, 1987.

> A print-out of the JOURLIT database, this is an index by key-word-in-title and author name to all articles in five major English-language psychoanalytic periodicals (listed in the JOURLIT listing earlier).

Watson, Robert I. *Eminent Contributors to Psychology*. New York: Springer, 1974-1976. 2 volumes.

DIRECTORIES

American Psychiatric Association. *Biographical Directory of the Fellows and Members of the American Psychiatric Association as of October 1977*. New York: Bowker, 1977.

American Psychological Association. *Biographical Directory*. Washington DC, 1948- .

Nordby, Vernon J., and Calvin S. Hall. *A Guide to Psychologists and Their Concepts*. San Francisco: W. H. Freeman, 1974.

OTHER USEFUL TOOLS

American Psychological Association. *Publication Manual*. 3d ed. Washington: American Psychological Association, 1983.

Explains the citation system and other stylistic matters for psychological journals, but not all psychoanalytic journals follow the APA Manual.

■ *Social Science Citation Index (SSCI)*. Philadelphia: Institute for Scientific Information, 1972.

Organized in a manner identical to the *Arts and Humanities Citation Index*, *SSCI* lists all the places where a given article or book is cited. It covers the broad spectrum of the social sciences, including psychology. Its particular value lies in the "keyword-in-title" approach provided by its *Permuterm Subject Index*; this allows identification of articles by a combination of their governing concepts and introduces a degree of specificity in subject searching not available elsewhere. With a retrospective five-year set published in 1979, coverage now extends from 1966 to the present. Contents of *SSCI* can also be searched on-line.

\# United States. National Clearinghouse for Mental Health Information. *Abstracts of the Standard Edition of the Complete Psychological Works of Sigmund Freud*. Ed. Carrie Lee Rothgeb. New York: International Universities Press, 1973. (Originally published by United States, Department of Health Education and Welfare, Superintendent of Documents, Stock Number 1724-0139.)

\# *The Concordance to the Standard Edition of the Complete Psychological Works of Sigmund Freud*. Ed. Samuel A. Guttman, Randall L. Jones, and Stephen M. Parrish. 6 volumes. Boston: G. K. Hall, 1980.

These are two especially useful reference tools for research on Freud's writings. The first furnishes brief summaries of all pieces included in the *Standard Edition*; these abstracts are supplemented by a keyword subject index to the summaries. The *Concordance* greatly enhances this keyword approach by analyzing appearances of all but the most nondistinctive words appearing in the English translation of Freud's words.

A pagination converter, provided in the *Concordance*, makes it possible to trace references in the English text to Freud's original German. The converter was originally published as "A Pagination Converter Relating the *Gesammelte Werke* to the *Standard Edition of the Complete Psychological Works of Sigmund Freud*," compiled by George H. Klumpner and Ernest S. Wolf, *International Journal of Psycho-Analysis* 52 (1971): 207-224.

\# United States. National Clearinghouse for Mental Health Information. *Abstracts of the Collected Works of C. G. Jung*. Ed.

Carrie Lee Rothgeb. Rockville MD: National Institute of Mental Health, 1978.

> Keyed to the *Collected Works of C. G. Jung* as published in the Bollingen Series XX by Princeton University Press, this tool provides summaries of Jung's papers and essays. A subject index provides "keyword" approaches to this material, thus making the body of Jung's writing accessible in considerable topical detail.

\# United States. National Clearinghouse for Mental Health Information. *Abstracts: The Psychoanalytic Study of the Child.* Ed. Carrie Lee Rothgeb. Rockville MD: National Institute of Mental Health, 1972.

> This tool abstracts materials published in the first twenty-five volumes of the annual, *The Psychoanalytic Study of the Child,* which since its inception in 1945 has become a major repository of psychoanalytic research. Complementing the abstracts are detailed author and subject indexes—the latter in a "keyword" format.

7

References

THIS LISTING includes only texts *both* referred to in Chapters 1-5 *and* useful (or amusing) to someone beginning to study psychoanalytic psychology or literature-and-psychology. It is *not* a list of everything worthwhile in those fields. (Fellow author, if your book is not in the list, that simply means it is beyond the introductory level.) Also, some writers referred to generally in Chapters 1-5 by way of history or background are not included here. For dictionaries, indexes, encyclopedias, and other bibliographic aids see Chapter 6.

Abbreviations: P = Press or Presses
                                 U = University or Universities

Abraham, Karl (1921). "Contributions to the Theory of the Anal Character." *Selected Papers on Psychoanalysis*. New York: Basic Books, 1953.

Alexander, Franz (1948). *Fundamentals of Psychoanalysis*. Rpt. New York: Norton, 1963.

Alpert, Judith L., ed. (1986). *Psychoanalysis and Women: Contemporary Reappraisals*. Hillsdale NJ: Analytic P.

Andersen, Wayne (1971). *Gauguin's Paradise Lost*. New York: Viking P.

Anderson, Richard C., Rand J. Spiro, and William E. Montague, eds. (1977). *Schooling and the Acquisition of Knowledge*. Hillsdale NJ: Lawrence Erlbaum.

Andrew, Dudley (1984). *Concepts in Film Theory*. New York: Oxford UP.

Appignanesi, Richard, and Oscar Zarate (1979). *Freud for Beginners*. New York: Pantheon.

Arlow, Jacob A., and Charles Brenner (1964). *Psychoanalytic Concepts and the Structural Theory*. New York: International UP.

Bär, Eugen S. (1974). "Understanding Lacan." *Psychoanalysis and Contemporary Science 3*. Leo Goldberger and Victor H. Rosen, eds. New York: International UP.

Barr, Marleen S., and Richard Feldstein, eds. (1989). *Discontented Discourses: Feminism / Textual Intervention / Psychoanalysis*. Urbana IL: U of Illinois P.

Beard, Ruth M. (1969). *An Outline of Piaget's Developmental Psychology for Students and Teachers*. New York: Mentor/New American Library.

Beardsley, Monroe, and W. K. Wimsatt, Jr. (1954). "The Affective Fallacy." W. K. Wimsatt, Jr., and Monroe Beardsley. *The Verbal Icon: Studies in the Meaning of Poetry.* Lexington: UP of Kentucky.

Beaugrande, Robert de (1980). *Text, Discourse, and Process.* London: Longman.

—— and Benjamin Colby (1979). "Narrative Models of Action and Interaction." *Cognitive Science* 3: 43-66.

Bellow, Saul (1965). *The Last Analysis.* New York: Viking P.

Belsky, Jay, ed. (1982). *In the Beginning: Readings on Infancy.* New York: Columbia UP.

Benvenuto, Bice, and Roger Kennedy (1986). *The Works of Jacques Lacan: An Introduction.* New York: St. Martin's P.

Berman, Jeffrey (1985). *The Talking Cure: Literary Representations of Psychoanalysis.* New York: New York UP.

Bernheimer, Charles, and Claire Kahane, eds. (1985). *In Dora's Case: Freud-Hysteria-Feminism.* New York: Columbia UP.

Bernstein, Anne E., and Gloria Marmar Warner (1981). *An Introduction to Contemporary Psychoanalysis.* New York: Jason Aronson.

Bersani, Leo (1977). *Baudelaire and Freud.* Berkeley: U of California P.

—— (1986). *The Freudian Body.* New York: Columbia UP.

Bibring, Edward (1941). "Zur Entwicklung und Problematik der Triebtheorie." *Imago* 22 (1936): 47-176. *Almanach der Psychoanalyse* (1937): 230-251. "The Development and Problems of the

Theory of the Instincts." *International Journal of Psycho-Analysis* 22 (1941): 102-131; rpt. 50 (1969): 293-308.

Bibring, Grete (1961). "A Study of Pregnancy." Appendix B, Glossary of Defenses. *The Psychoanalytic Study of the Child* 14: 62-71.

Bleich, David (1975). *Readings and Feelings: An Introduction to Subjective Criticism*. Urbana IL: National Council of Teachers of English.

—— (1977). *Literature and Self-Awareness: Critical Questions and Emotional Responses*. New York: Harper and Row.

—— (1978). *Subjective Criticism*. Baltimore: Johns Hopkins UP.

—— (1988). *The Double Perspective: Language, Literacy, and Social Relations*. New York: Oxford UP.

—— et al. (1978). "The Psychological Study of Language and Literature: A Selected Annotated Bibliography." *Style* 12: 113-210.

Bloom, Harold (1973). *The Anxiety of Influence: A Theory of Poetry*. New York: Oxford UP.

Bodkin, Maud (1934, 1963). *Archetypal Patterns in Poetry*. New York and London: Oxford UP.

Bollas, Christopher (1987). *The Shadow of the Object: Psychoanalysis of the Unthought Known*. New York: Columbia UP.

Bonaparte, Marie, Princess (1933). *Edgar Poe, Étude Psychanalytique*. Paris: Denöel et Steele.

Bordwell, David (1985). *Narration in the Fiction Film*. Madison WI: U of Wisconsin P.

Brenner, Charles (1973). *An Elementary Textbook of Psychoanalysis*. Rev. ed. New York: International UP.

Buckley, Peter, ed. (1986). *Essential Papers on Object Relations*. New York: New York UP.

Burke, Kenneth (1941). "Freud and the Analysis of Poetry." *The Philosophy of Literary Form: Studies in Symbolic Action*. Baton Rouge: Louisiana State UP.

—— (1966). "Shakespearean Persuasion - *Antony and Cleopatra*." "*Coriolanus* - and the Delights of Faction." "'Kubla Khan,' Proto-Surrealist Poem." *Language as Symbolic Action: Essays on Life, Literature, and Method*. Berkeley: U of California P.

Burnham, John (1978). "The Influence of Psychoanalysis Upon American Culture." *American Psychoanalysis: Origins and Development*. Jacques Quen and Eric T. Carlson, eds. The Adolf Meyer Seminars. New York: Brunner/Mazel. 52-72.

Bush, Marshall (1967). "The Problem of Form in the Psychoanalytic Theory of Art." *Psychoanalytic Review* 54: 5-35.

Buttonwieser, Paul (1981). *Free Association*. Boston: Little, Brown.

Buxbaum, Edith (1959). "Psychosexual Development: The Oral, Anal, and Phallic Phases." *Readings in Psychoanalytic Psychology*. Morton Levitt, ed. New York: Appleton-Century-Crofts, 1959. 43-55.

Chodorow, Nancy (1978). *The Reproduction of Mothering: Psychoanalysis and the Sociology of Gender*. Berkeley: U of California P.

Cixous, Hélène (1975). "Le Rire de la Medusa." *L'Arc* 39-54. "The Laugh of the Medusa." Trans. Keith Cohen and Paula Cohen. *Signs* 1.4 (1976): 875-893.

—— and Catherine Clément (1986). *The Newly Born Woman. (La Jeune née.)* Trans. Betsy Wing. Minneapolis: U of Minnesota P.

Clément, Catherine (1983). *Vies et légendes de Jacques Lacan.* Paris: Éditions Bernard Grasset. *The Lives and Legends of Jacques Lacan.* Trans. Arthur Goldhammer. New York: Columbia UP.

Crews, Frederick, ed. (1970). *Psychoanalysis and Literary Process.* Cambridge MA: Winthrop Publishers.

Crowder, Robert G. (1982). *The Psychology of Reading: An Introduction.* New York: Oxford UP.

Davies, John Booth (1978). *The Psychology of Music.* Stanford CA: Stanford UP.

Davis, Robert Con, ed. (1981). *The Fictional Father: Lacanian Readings of the Text.* Amherst: U of Massachusetts P.

De Lauretis, Teresa (1984). *Alice Doesn't: Feminism, Semiotics, Cinema.* Bloomington IN: Indiana UP.

Derwin, Daniel (1985). *Through a Freudian Lens Deeply: A Psychoanalysis of Cinema.* Hillsdale NJ: Lawrence Erlbaum.

Diesing, Paul (1971). *Patterns of Discovery in the Social Sciences.* Chicago: Aldine-Atherton.

Dillon, George L. (1978). *Language Processing and the Reading of Literature: Toward a Model of Comprehension.* Bloomington IN: Indiana UP.

Eagle, Morris N. (1984). *Recent Developments in Psychoanalysis*. New York: McGraw-Hill.

Edel, Leon (1953-1972). *Henry James*. 5 vols. Philadelphia: Lippincott.

—— (1959). *Literary Biography*. Garden City: Doubleday-Anchor.

—— (1973). "Towards a Theory of Literary Psychology." *Interpersonal Explorations in Psychoanalysis*. Ed. Earl G. Wittenberg. New York: Basic Books. 343-354.

—— (1981). "The Nature of Literary Psychology." *Journal of the American Psychoanalytic Association* 29.2: 447-467.

Edelson, Marshall (1972). "Language and Dreams: *The Interpretation of Dreams* Revisited." *The Psychoanalytic Study of the Child* 27: 203-282.

Ehrenzweig, Anton (1967). *The Hidden Order of Art: A Study in the Psychology of Artistic Imagination*. Berkeley: U of California P.

Ellenbogen, Glenn C., ed. (1986). *Oral Sadism and the Vegetarian Personality*. Readings from the *Journal of Polymorphous Perversity*. A Stonesong Press Book. New York: Brunner/Mazel.

Empson, William (1935). *Some Versions of Pastoral*. London: Chatto & Windus.

Erdelyi, Matthew Hugh (1985). *Psychoanalysis: Freud's Cognitive Psychology*. New York: W. H. Freeman.

Erikson, Erik H. (1954). "The Dream Specimen of Psychoanalysis." *Journal of the American Psychoanalytic Association* 2 (1954): 5-56. Rev. *Identity: Youth and Crisis*. New York: Norton, 1968.

—— (1963). *Childhood and Society*. 2d ed. New York: Norton.

—— (1976a). "Reflections on Dr. Borg's Life Cycle." *Daedalus* 105.2: 1-28.

—— (1976b). *Identity: Youth and Crisis*. New York: Norton. 142-150, 188-89.

Fairbairn, W. Ronald D. (1963). "Synopsis of an Object-Relations Theory of the Personality." *International Journal of Psycho-Analysis* 44: 224-225.

Feder, Stuart, Richard L. Karmel, and George H. Pollock, eds. (1989). *Psychoanalytic Explorations of Music*. New York: International UP.

Feldstein, Richard, and Judith Roof (1989). *Feminism and Psychoanalysis*. Ithaca NY: Cornell UP.

Felman, Shoshana (1978). *La folie et la chose littéraire*. Paris: Seuil.

—— (1987). *Jacques Lacan and the Adventure of Insight: Psychoanalysis in Contemporary Culture*. Paris: Seuil.

——, ed. (1982). *Literature and Psychoanalysis: The Question of Reading: Otherwise*. Baltimore: Johns Hopkins UP.

Fenichel, Otto. (1931). "Specific Forms of the Oedipus Complex." *Collected Papers: First Series*. New York: Norton, 1953. 204-220.

—— (1945). *The Psychoanalytic Theory of Neurosis*. New York: Norton.

Fetterley, Judith (1978). *The Resisting Reader: A Feminist Approach to American Fiction*. Bloomington: Indiana UP.

Fiedler, Leslie A. (1960). *Love and Death in the American Novel*. New York: Criterion Books.

Fischer, Jens Malte, ed. (1980). *Psychoanalytische Literatur-interpretation*. Tübingen: Max Niemayer Verlag.

Fish, Stanley (1967). *Surprised by Sin: The Reader in* Paradise Lost. London and New York: St. Martin's P.

—— (1980). *Is There a Text in this Class? The Authority of Interpretive Communities*. Cambridge MA: Harvard UP.

Fisher, Seymour, and Roger P. Greenberg (1977). *The Scientific Credibility of Freud's Theories and Therapy*. New York: Basic Books.

Fletcher, Angus (1964). *Allegory: The Theory of a Symbolic Mode*. Ithaca NY: Cornell UP.

Flynn, Elizabeth A., and Patrocinio P. Schwieckart, eds. (1986). *Gender and Reading: Essays on Readers, Texts, and Contexts*. Baltimore and London: Johns Hopkins UP.

Franzosa, John C., Jr. (1973). "Criticism and the Uses of Psycho-analysis." *College English* 34 (1973): 927-933.

Freud, Sigmund (1953-1974). *The Standard Edition of the Complete Psychological Works*. Trans. and ed. James Strachey in collaboration with Anna Freud, assisted by Alix Strachey and Alan Tyson. 24 vols. London: The Hogarth Press and the Institute of Psycho-Analysis, 1953-1974. All subsequent references to Freud's works are to volume and page in this edition. The letters after the date refer to the "Freud Bibliography" in Volume 24 of the *Standard Edition*, pp. 47-82, which gives complete bibliographical information for English and German editions.

—— (1900a). *The Interpretation of Dreams*. 4-5: 1-627.

—— (1905c). *Jokes and Their Relation to the Unconscious*. 8: 3-236.

—— (1905d). *Three Essays on the Theory of Sexuality*. 7: 125-243.

—— (1908b). "Character and Anal Erotism." 9: 169-175.

—— (1908e). "Creative Writers and Day Dreaming." 9: 142-153.

—— (1911b). "Formulations on the Two Principles of Mental Functioning." 12: 215-226.

—— (1915e). "The Unconscious." 14: 161-215.

—— (1915-1916). *Introductory Lectures on Psycho-Analysis*. 15: 3-16: 476.

—— (1920g). *Beyond the Pleasure Principle*. 18: 7-64.

—— (1923b). *The Ego and the Id*. 19: 3-66.

—— (1933a). *New Introductory Lectures on Psycho-Analysis*. 22: 3-182.

—— (1986). *The Essentials of Psychoanalysis*. Anna Freud, ed. London: Hogarth P.

—— (1989). *The Freud Reader*. Peter Gay, ed. New York: Norton.

Freud. Writ., Carey Harrison. Prod., John Purdie. BBC-TV Production. Hearst/ABC-KCTV, n.d.

Freund, Elizabeth (1987). *The Return of the Reader: Reader-response Criticism*. New York and London: Methuen.

Friedan, Betty (1963). *The Feminine Mystique*. New York: Norton.

Fromm, Erich (1947). *Man for Himself: An Inquiry into the Psychology of Ethics*. New York: Rinehart.

Fruman, Norman (1971). *Coleridge, the Damaged Archangel*. New York: Braziller.

Frye, Northrop (1957). *Anatomy of Criticism*. Princeton NJ: Princeton UP.

Fuller, Peter (1980). *Art and Psychoanalysis*. London: Writers and Readers Cooperative.

Gabbard, Krin, and Glen O. (1987). *Psychiatry and the Cinema: A Dual Perspective*. Chicago: U of Chicago P.

Gallop, Jane (1982). *The Daughter's Seduction: Feminism and Psychoanalysis*. Ithaca NY: Cornell UP.

Gardiner, Judith Kegan (1976). "Psychoanalytic Criticism and the Female Reader." *Literature and Psychology* 26 (1976): 100-107.

Gardner, Howard (1973). *The Arts and Human Development*. New York: Wiley.

—— (1985). *The Mind's New Science: A History of the Cognitive Revolution*. New York: Basic Books.

Garner, Shirley Nelson, Claire Kahane, and Madelon Sprengnether, eds. (1985). *The (M)other Tongue: Essays in Feminist Psychoanalytic Interpretation*. Ithaca NY: Cornell UP, 1985.

Gelfand, Elissa D., and Virgina Thorndike Hules (1985). *French Feminist Criticism: Women, Language, and Literature, An Annotated Bibliography*. New York and London: Garland.

Gilbert, Sandra M., and Susan Gubar (1979). *The Madwoman in the Attic: The Woman Writer and the Nineteenth-Century Literary Imagination*. New Haven and London: Yale UP.

—— (1988-). *No Man's Land: The Place of the Woman Writer in the Twentieth Century*. 3 vols. New Haven and London: Yale UP. Vol. 1: *The War of the Words* (1988). Vol. 2: *Sexchanges* (1989).

Gilman, Sander L., ed. (1982). *Introducing Psychoanalytic Theory*. New York: Bruner/Mazel.

Gombrich, E. H. (1954). "Psycho-Analysis and the History of Art." *Meditations on a Hobby Horse*. London: Phaidon, 1963.

—— (1977). *Art and Illusion: A Study in the Psychology of Pictorial Representation*. 5th ed., rev. New York: Bollingen Foundation and Pantheon Books.

—— (1978). *Meditations on a Hobby Horse, and Other Essays on the Theory of Art*. 3d ed. London: Phaidon.

—— (1982). *The Image and the Eye: Further Studies in the Psychology of Pictorial Representation*. Ithaca NY: Cornell UP.

Grant, Audrey N. (1987). *Young Readers Reading*. Melbourne: Routledge and Kegan Paul.

Greenacre, Phyllis (1955). *Swift and Carroll: A Psychoanalytic Study of Two Lives*. New York, International UP.

Greenberg, Harvey (1975). *Movies on Your Mind*. New York: Dutton.

Greenberg, Jay R., and Stephen A. Mitchell (1983). *Object Relations in Psychoanalytic Theory*. Cambridge MA: Harvard UP.

Grimaud, Michel (1976). "Recent Trends in Psychoanalysis: A Survey with Emphasis on Psychological Criticism in English Literature and Related Areas." *Sub-Stance*, no. 13: 136-162.

—— (1980). "Psychology, Language, Esthetics, Computers: Critical Notes." *Sub-Stance*, no. 25: 111-117.

—— (1982). "Part Three: A Reader's Guide to Psychoanalysis. An Overview of Psychoanalytic Theory and the Psychoanalytic Approach in Literary Theory and Practice, with Emphasis on French Studies." William J. Berg, Michel Grimaud, and George Moskos. *Saint/Oedipus: Psychocritical Approaches to Flaubert's Art*. Ithaca NY: Cornell UP. 271-88.

—— (1984). "Poetics from Psychoanalysis to Cognitive Psychology." *Poetics* 13: 325-345.

Grolnick, Simon A., and Leonard Barkin, eds., with Werner Muensterberger (1978). *Between Reality and Fantasy: Transitional Objects and Phenomena*. New York: Jason Aronson.

Grosskurth, Phyllis (1986). *Melanie Klein: Her World and Her Work*. New York: Knopf.

Guntrip, Harry (1969). "Four Phases of Psychodynamic Theory." *Schizoid Phenomena, Object Relations and the Self*. New York: International UP.

Harding, Sandra, and Merrill B. Hintikka, eds. (1983). *Discovering Reality: Feminist Perspectives on Epistemology, Metaphysics, Methodology, and Philosophy of Science*. Dordrecht, Holland: D. Reidel.

Harris, Jay E. (1986). *Clinical Neuroscience: From Neuroanatomy to Psychodynamics*. New York: Human Sciences P.

Hartman, Geoffrey, ed. (1978). *Psychoanalysis and the Question of the Text*. Baltimore: Johns Hopkins UP.

Hartmann, Heinz (1939). "Ich-Psychologie und Anpassungs-Problem." *Internationale Zeitschrift für Psychanalyse* 24: 62-135. *Ego Psychology and the Problem of Adaptation*. Trans. David Rapaport. *Journal of the American Psychoanalytic Association*, Monograph No. 1. New York: International UP, 1958.

—— (1964). *Essays on Ego Psychology: Selected Problems in Psychoanalytic Theory*. New York: International UP.

Heath, Stephen (1981). *Questions of Cinema*. Bloomington: Indiana UP.

Hendrick, Ives (1958). *Facts and Theories of Psychoanalysis*. 3d. ed. New York: Dell Publishing Co..

Hillman, James (1975). *Re-Visioning Psychology*. New York: Harper & Row.

—— (1983). *Archetypal Psychology*. Dallas: Spring Publication.

—— and Charles Boer, eds. (1985). *Freud's Own Cookbook*. New York: Harper and Row.

Hoffman, Frederick J. (1945). *Freudianism and the Literary Mind*. Baton Rouge: Louisiana State UP. 2d ed. 1957.

Holland, Norman N. (1966). "Freud on the Artist." "Freud on the Work." "Freud on the Response." "And Beside Freud." *Psychoanalysis and Shakespeare*. New York: McGraw-Hill, chs. 2-5, pp. 9-52.

—— (1968). *The Dynamics of Literary Response*. New York: Oxford UP.

—— (1975a). "Unity Identity Text Self." *PMLA* 90: 813-822.

—— (1975b). *5 Readers Reading*. New Haven and London: Yale UP.

—— (1976a). "Literary Interpretation and Three Phases of Psycho-analysis." *Critical Inquiry* 3: 221-233.

—— (1976b). "Transactive Criticism: Re-creation Through Identity." *Criticism* 18: 334-352.

—— (1977). "Transactive Teaching: Cordelia's Death." *College English* 39: 276-285.

—— (1978a). "Literary Interpretation and Three Phases of Psycho-analysis." *Psychoanalysis, Creativity, and Literature: A French-American Inquiry.* Alan Roland, ed. New York: Columbia UP, pp. 233-247.

—— (1978b). With the members of English 692: Colloquium in Psy-choanalytic Criticism. "Poem Opening: An Invitation to Trans-active Criticism." *College English* 40: 2-16.

—— (1982). *Laughing: A Psychology of Humor.* Ithaca NY: Cor-nell UP.

—— (1985). *The I.* New Haven and London: Yale UP.

—— (1986a). "Twenty-Five Years and Thirty Days." *Psychoanalytic Quarterly* 55: 23-52.

—— (1986b). "I-ing Film." *Critical Inquiry* 12: 654-671.

—— (1986c). "The Miller's Wife and the Professors: Questions about the Transactive Theory of Reading." *New Literary History* 17: 423-447.

—— (1988). *The Brain of Robert Frost.* New York and London: Routledge.

—— and Murray Schwartz (1975). "The Delphi Seminar." *College English* 36: 789-800.

Holub, Robert C. (1984). *Reception Theory: A Critical Introduction.* London and New York: Methuen.

Hopper, Stanley, and David Miller, eds. (1967). *Interpretation: Poetry of Meaning.* New York: Harcourt, Brace, and World.

Horney, Karen (1939). *New Ways in Psychoanalysis.* New York: Norton.

—— (1945). *Our Inner Conflicts: A Constructive Theory of Neurosis.* New York: Norton.

—— (1950). *Neurosis and Human Growth: The Struggle toward Self-Realization.* New York: Norton.

—— (1967). *Feminine Psychology.* Ed. and introd. Harold Kelman. New York: Norton.

Hughes, Judith M. (1989). *Reshaping the Psychoanalytic Domain: The Work of Melanie Klein, W. R. D. Fairbairn, and D. W. Winnicott.* Berkeley: U of California P.

Irigaray, Luce (1974). *Speculum de l'Autre Femme.* Paris: Éditions de Minuit. *Speculum of the Other Woman.* Trans. Gillian C. Gill. Ithaca NY: Cornell UP, 1985.

—— (1977). *Ce sexe qui n'en pas un.* Paris: Éditions de Minuit. *This Sex Which Is Not One.* Trans. Catherine Porter with Carolyn Burke. Ithaca NY: Cornell UP, 1985.

Johnson, Mark (1987). *The Body in the Mind: The Bodily Basis of Reason and Imagination.* Chicago and London: U of Chicago P.

Jones, Ernest (1916). "The Theory of Symbolism." *Papers on Psycho-Analysis*. 5th ed. London: Baillière, Tindall, and Cox, 1948. 87-144.

—— (1918). "Anal-Erotic Character Traits." *Papers on Psycho-Analysis*. 5th ed. London: Baillière, Tindall, and Cox, 1948. 413-437.

—— (1953-57). *The Life and Work of Sigmund Freud*. 3 Vols. New York: Basic Books.

—— ([1910]1949). *Hamlet and Oedipus*. New York: Norton.

Jose, Paul E., and William F. Brewer (1984). "Development of Story Liking: Character Identification, Suspense, and Outcome Resolution." *Developmental Psychology* 20: 911-924.

Jung, Carl Gustav (1953-1983). *Collected Works*. Ed. Sir Herbert Read, Michael Fordham, and Gerhard Adler. Bollingen Series XX. New York: Pantheon, 1953-1966. Princeton NJ: Princeton UP, 1966-1983.

Kaplan, E. Ann, ed. (1989). *Psychoanalysis and Cinema*. New York and London: Routledge.

Kaplan, Justin (1966). *Mr. Clemens and Mark Twain: A Biography*. New York: Simon and Schuster.

—— (1982). *Walt Whitman: A Life*. New York: Simon and Schuster.

Kaplan, Morton, and Robert Kloss, eds. (1973). *The Unspoken Motive: A Guide to Psychoanalytic Literary Criticism*. New York: Free P.

Kernberg, Otto (1975). *Borderline Conditions and Pathological Narcissism*. New York: Jason Aronson.

—— (1978). *Object-Relations Theory and Clinical Psychoanalysis*. New York: Jason Aronson.

—— (1980). *Internal World and External Reality: Object Relations Theory Applied*. New York and London: Jason Aronson.

Klein, Melanie (1975). "The Importance of Symbol-Formation in the Development of the Ego" (1930). *Complete Works*. 5 vols. London: Hogarth P. 1: 219-232.

Kline, Paul (1972). *Fact and Fantasy in Freudian Theory*. London: Methuen.

Koffka, Kurt (1935). *Principles of Gestalt Psychology*. New York: Harcourt, Brace.

Kohon, Gregorio, ed. (1986). *The British School of Psychoanalysis: The Independent Tradition*. New Haven and London: Yale UP.

Kohut, Heinz (1971). *The Analysis of the Self*. New York: International UP.

—— (1977). *The Restoration of the Self*. New York: International UP.

—— and Ernest S. Wolf (1978). "The Disorders of the Self and Their Treatment: An Outline." *International Journal of Psycho-Analysis* 59: 413-425.

Kris, Ernst (1952). *Psychoanalytic Explorations in Art*. New York: International UP.

Kristeva, Julia (1980). *Pouvoirs de l'Horreur*. Paris: Éditions du Seuil. *Powers of Horror: An Essay on Abjection*. Trans. Leon S. Roudiez. New York: Columbia UP, 1982.

—— (1986). *The Kristeva Reader*. Ed. Toril Moi. New York: Columbia UP.

Kugler, Paul (1982). *The Alchemy of Discourse: An Archetypal Approach to Language*. Lewisburg PA: Bucknell UP.

Kutash, Emilie F. Sobel (1982). "A Psychoanalytic Approach to Understanding Form in Abstract Expressionist and Minimalist Painting." *International Review of Psycho-Analysis* 9: 167-177.

Laberge, David, and S. Jay Samuels, eds. (1977). *Basic Processes in Reading: Perception and Comprehension*. New York: Lawrence Erlbaum.

Lacan, Jacques (1949). "Le Stade du miroir comme formateur de la fonction du Je, telle qu'elle nous est révélée dans l'expérience psychanalytique." *Revue Française de Psychanalyse* 13: 449-455. *Écrits: A Selection*. Trans. Alan Sheridan. New York: Norton, 1977. 1-7.

—— (1956a). "Fonction et champ de la parole et du langage en psychanalyse." *La Psychanalyse* 1: 81-166. "The Function and Field of Speech and Language in Psychoanalysis." *Écrits: A Selection*. Trans. Alan Sheridan. New York: Norton, 1977. 30-113.

—— (1956b). "Le séminaire sur 'La lettre volée.'" *La Psychanalyse* 2: 1-44. Trans. Jeffrey Mehlman. *Yale French Studies* 48 (1972): 38-72.

—— (1957). "L'instance de la lettre dans l'inconscient ou la raison depuis Freud." *La Psychanalyse* 3: 47-81. "The Agency of the Letter in the Unconscious or Reason Since Freud." *Écrits: A Selection*. Trans. Alan Sheridan. New York: Norton, 1977. 146-178.

—— (1958). "La signification du phallus." *Écrits*. Paris: Éditions du Seuil, 1966. 685-695. "The Signification of the Phallus." *Écrits: A Selection*. Trans. Alan Sheridan. New York: Norton, 1977. 281-291.

—— (1959). "Desire and the Interpretation of Desire in *Hamlet*." *Literature and Psychoanalysis: The Question of Reading: Otherwise*. Shoshana Felman, ed. Baltimore: Johns Hopkins UP, 1977. 11-52.

—— (1966). *Écrits* Paris: Éditions du Seuil, 1966. Partially translated and reprinted in *Écrits: A Selection*. Trans. Alan Sheridan. New York: Norton, 1977.

—— (1975-). *Le séminaire de Jacques Lacan (1953-1975)*. Texte établi par Jacques-Alain Miller. Paris: Éditions du Seuil. Livre 1: *Les écrits techniques de Freud* (1953-1954). Livre 2: *Le moi dans la theorie de Freud et dans la technique de la psychanalyse* (1954-1955). No. 3: *Les psychoses* (1955-1956). No. 8: *Le transfert* (1961). Livre 11: *Les quatre concepts fondamentaux de la psychanalyse* (1964). Livre 20: *Encore* (1973). *The Seminar of Jacques Lacan*. Jacques-Alain Miller, ed. New York: Norton, 1988- ; Cambridge: Cambridge UP, 1988- . Book 1: *Freud's Papers on Technique* (1953-1954). Trans. Sylvana Tomaselli and John Forrester. Book 2: *The Ego in Freud's Theory and in the Technique of Psychoanalysis* (1954-1955). Trans. Sylvana Tomaselli and John Forrester.

—— (1977). *The Four Fundamental Concepts of Psycho-analysis*. Jacques-Alain Miller, ed. Trans. Alan Sheridan. The International Psycho-analytical Library, No. 106. London: Hogarth P. Translation of *Le séminaire* (1975-), vol. 11. New York: Norton, 1978.

—— (1987). *Joyce avec Lacan*. Jacques Aubert, ed. Paris: Navarin Éditeur.

Lagache, Daniel (1971). *La psychanalyse*. Paris: Presses Universitaires de France. *Psychoanalysis*. Trans. Beatrice Scott. 2d rev. French ed. New York: Walker, 1963.

Laing, R. D. (1965). *The Divided Self: An Existential Study in Sanity and Madness*. Baltimore: Penguin.

Lakoff, George (1987). *Women, Fire, and Dangerous Things: What Categories Reveal About the Mind*. Chicago and London: U of Chicago P.

—— and Mark Johnson (1980). *Metaphors We Live By*. Chicago and London: U of Chicago P.

Laplanche, Jean (1976). *Life and Death in Psychoanalysis*. Trans. Jeffrey Mehlman. Baltimore: Johns Hopkins UP.

—— and J.-B. Pontalis (1968). *Vocabulaire de la Psychanalyse*. Paris: Presses Universitaires de France. *The Language of Psycho-Analysis*. Trans. Donald Nicholson-Smith. New York: Norton, 1973.

Laughlin, H. P. (1979). *The Ego and Its Defenses*. 2d ed. New York: Jason Aronson.

Layton, Lynne, and Barbara Ann Schapiro, eds. (1986). *Narcissism and the Text: Studies in Literature and the Psychology of Self*. New York and London: New York UP.

Lebeaux, Richard Mark (1977). *Young Man Thoreau*. Amherst MA: U of Massachusetts P.

Lemaire, Anika (1977). *Jacques Lacan*. Trans. David Macey. Boston: Routledge and Kegan Paul.

Lenz, Carolyn Ruth Swift, Gayle Greene, and Carol Thomas Neely, eds. (1980). *The Woman's Part: Feminist Criticism of Shakespeare*. Urbana IL: U of Illinois P.

Lesser, Simon O. (1957). *Fiction and the Unconscious*. Boston: Beacon P.

Lewin, Bertram D. (1933). "The Body as Phallus." *Psychoanalytic Quarterly* 2: 24-47.

Lichtenstein, Heinz (1961). "Identity and Sexuality: A Study of Their Interrelationship in Man." *Journal of the American Psychoanalytic Association* 9: 179-260. Rev. "Identity and Sexuality." *The Dilemma of Human Identity*. New York: Jason Aronson, 1977. 49-122.

—— (1963). "The Dilemma of Human Identity: Notes on Self Transformation, Self-Objectification, and Metamorphosis." *Journal of the American Psychoanalytic Association* 11: 172-223. Rev. *The Dilemma of Human Identity*. New York: Jason Aronson, 1977. 141-204.

—— (1977). *The Dilemma of Human Identity*. New York: Jason Aronson.

Mahler, Margaret, Fred Pine, and Anni Bergman (1975). *The Psychological Birth of the Human Infant: Symbiosis and Individuation*. New York: Basic Books.

Malcolm, Janet (1981). *Psychoanalysis: The Impossible Profession*. New York: Knopf.

—— (1984). *In the Freud Archives*. New York: Knopf.

Malzberg, Barry N. (1985). *The Remaking of Sigmund Freud*. New York: Ballantine/Del Rey.

Manheim, Leonard F., and Eleanor Manheim (1966). *Hidden Patterns: Studies in Psychoanalytic Literary Criticism*. New York: Macmillan.

Marks, Elaine, and Isabelle de Courtivron, eds. (1980). *New French Feminisms: An Anthology*. Amherst MA: U of Massachusetts P.

Maslow, Abraham H. (1968). *Toward a Psychology of Being*. 2d ed. New York: Van Nostrand.

—— (1970). *Motivation and Personality*. 2d ed. New York: Harper and Row.

Mast, Gerald, and Marshall Cohen, eds. (1985). *Film Theory and Criticism*. 3d ed. New York: Oxford UP.

Mauron, Charles (1963). *Des Métaphores obsédantes au mythe personnel*. Paris: José Corti.

Mazlish, Bruce (1970). "Autobiography and Psycho-analysis." *Encounter* (October): 28-37.

Meek, Margaret, et al. (1982). *Learning to Read*. London: Bodley Head.

—— et al. (1983). *Achieving Literacy: Longitudinal Studies of Adolescents Learning To Read*. London and Boston: Routledge and Kegan Paul.

—— et al. (1985). *Opening Moves: Work in Progress in the Study of Children's Language Development*. Bedford Way Papers 17. London: Institute of Education, University of London.

Mehlman, Jeffrey, ed. (1972). *French Freud: Structural Studies in Psychoanalysis*. *Yale French Studies* 48.

Meissner, W. W. (1966). "The Operational Principle and Meaning in Psychoanalysis." *Psychoanalytic Quarterly* 35: 233-255.

—— (1970). "Notes on Identification." *Psychoanalytic Quarterly* 39: 563-589; 40 (1971): 277-302; 41 (1972): 224-260.

—— (1971). "Freud's Methodology." *Journal of the American Psychoanalytic Association* 19: 265-309.

Metz, Christian (1982). *Le signifiant imaginaire*. Paris: Union Générale d'Éditions, 1977. *The Imaginary Signifier: Psychoanalysis and the Cinema*. Trans. Celia Britton et al. Bloomington: Indiana UP.

Meyer, Bernard C. (1967). *Joseph Conrad: A Psychoanalytic Biography*. Princeton NJ: Princeton UP.

—— (1976). *Houdini: A Mind in Chains: A Psychoanalytic Portrait*. New York: Dutton.

Michaels, Joseph (1955). *Disorders of Character: Persistent Enuresis, Juvenile Delinquency, and Psychopathic Personality*. Springfield IL: Charles C. Thomas.

Millett, Kate (1970). *Sexual Politics*. Garden City NY: Doubleday.

Milner, Marion [Joanna Field] (1957). *On Not Being Able to Paint*. 2d ed. New York: International UP.

Mitchell, Juliet (1974). *Psychoanalysis and Feminism: Freud, Reich, Laing, and Women*. New York: Pantheon.

—— and Jacqueline Rose, eds. (1982). *Feminine Sexuality: Jacques Lacan and the école freudienne.* Trans. Jacqueline Rose. London: Macmillan.

Moi, Toril, ed. (1987). *French Feminist Thought: A Reader.* Oxford and New York: Blackwell.

Moore, Burness E., and Bernard D. Fine (1967). *A Glossary of Psychoanalytic Terms and Concepts.* New York: American Psychoanalytic Association.

Morrison, Claudia C. (1968). *Freud and the Critic: The Early Use of Depth Psychology in Literary Criticism.* Chapel Hill: U of North Carolina P.

Muller, John P., and William J. Richardson (1982). *Lacan and Language: A Reader's Guide to "Écrits."* New York: International UP.

Mulvey, Laura (1975). "Visual Pleasure and the Narrative Cinema." *Screen* 16.3 (Autumn): 6-18.

Münsterberg, Hugo (1916). *The Photoplay: A Psychological Study.* New York: D. Appleton. Rpt. *The Film: A Psychological Study.* New York: Dover, 1970.

Natoli, Joseph, and Frederik L. Rusch, comps. (1984). *Psychocriticism: An Annotated Bibliography.* Bibliographies and Indexes in World Literature, Number 1. Westport CT and London: Greenwood P.

Nichols, Bill, ed. (1976). *Movies and Methods: An Anthology.* Berkeley: U of California P.

Noland, Richard (1979). "The Theory of the Crisis of Generativity in Sophocles' *Oedipus the King.*" *Hartford Studies in Literature* 11: 83-93.

Noy, Pinchas (1966-67). "The Psychodynamic Meaning of Music: A Critical Review of the Psychoanalytic and Related Literature." *Journal of Music Therapy* 3.4: 126-34; 4.1: 7-23; 4.2: 45-51; 4.3: 81-94; 4.4: 117-125.

—— (1969). "A Revision of the Psychoanalytic Theory of the Primary Process." *International Journal of Psycho-Analysis* 50: 155-178.

—— (1979). "Form Creation in Art: An Ego-Psychological Approach to Creativity." *Psychoanalytic Quarterly* 48 (1979): 229-256.

Ornstein, Paul H. (1974). "On Narcissism: Beyond the Introduction; Highlights of Heinz Kohut's Contributions to the Psychoanalytic Treatment of Narcissistic Disorders." *Annual of Psychoanalysis* 2: 127-149.

Palombo, Stanley R. (1978). *Dreaming and Memory: A New Information-Processing Model.* New York: Basic Books.

Paris, Bernard J. (1974). *A Psychological Approach to Fiction: Studies in Thackeray, Stendhal, George Eliot, Dostoevsky, and Conrad.* Bloomington: Indiana UP.

—— (1986). "Horney, Maslow, and the Third Force." *Third Force Psychology and the Study of Literature.* Rutherford NJ: Fairleigh Dickinson UP. 25-60.

——, ed. (1986). *Third Force Psychology and the Study of Literature.* Rutherford NJ: Fairleigh Dickinson UP.

Peckham, Morse (1965). *Man's Rage for Chaos: Biology, Behavior, and the Arts.* Philadelphia and New York: Chilton Books.

Penley, Constance, ed. (1988). *Feminism and Film Theory.* New York and London: Routledge.

Perkins, David, and Barbara Leondar, eds. (1977). *The Arts and Cognition.* Baltimore: Johns Hopkins UP.

Peterfreund, Emanuel (1980). "On Information and Systems Models for Psychoanalysis." *International Review of Psycho-Analysis* 7: 327-345.

Phillips, William, ed. (1957). *Art and Psychoanalysis.* New York: Criterion Books.

Piaget, Jean (1951). *Play, Dreams and Imitation in Childhood.* London: Heinemann.

Purves, Alan C., and Richard Beach (1972). *Literature and the Reader: Research in Response to Literature, Reading Interests, and the Teaching of Literature.* Urbana IL: National Council of Teachers of English.

Quen, Jacques, and Eric T. Carlson, eds. (1978). *American Psychoanalysis: Origins and Development.* The Adolf Meyer Seminars. New York: Brunner/Mazel.

Ragland-Sullivan, Ellie (1986). *Jacques Lacan and the Philosophy of Psychoanalysis.* Urbana and Chicago: U of Illinois P.

Rank, Otto (1926). *Das Inzestmotiv in Dichtung und Sage.* Vienna: Deuticke.

—— (1932). *Art and Artist: Creative Urge and Personality Development.* New York: Knopf.

Rapaport, David (1959). "Introduction: A Historical Survey of Psychoanalytic Ego Psychology." *Psychological Issues*, Vol. 1, No. 1, Monograph 1. New York: International UP.

—— and Merton M. Gill (1959). "The Points of View and Assumptions of Metapsychology." *International Journal of Psycho-Analysis* 40: 153-162.

Read, Herbert Edward, Sir (1967). *Poetry and Experience*. New York: Horizon P.

Reich, Wilhelm (1949). *Character Analysis*. 3d ed. New York: Noonday.

Reppen, Joseph, ed. (1981). "Symposium: Emanuel Peterfreund on Information and Systems Theory." *Psychoanalytic Review* 68: 159-190.

——, ed. (1985). *Beyond Freud: A Study of Modern Psychoanalytic Theorists*. Hillsdale NJ: Analytic P/ Lawrence Erlbaum.

Richards, I. A. (1924). *Principles of Literary Criticism*. Cambridge: Cambridge UP.

—— (1929). *Practical Criticism*. Cambridge: Cambridge UP.

Rogers, Carl R. (1961). *On Becoming a Person: A Therapist's View of Psychotherapy*. Boston: Houghton Mifflin.

Rogers, Robert (1978). *Metaphor: A Psychoanalytic View*. Berkeley: U of California P.

Rose, Gilbert (1980). *The Power of Form: A Psychoanalytic Approach to Aesthetic Form*. Psychological Issues, Monograph 49. New York: International UP.

Rosen, Philip, ed. (1986). *Narrative, Apparatus, Ideology: A Film Theory Reader.* New York: Columbia UP.

Rosenblatt, Louise M. (1937). *Literature as Exploration.* 4th ed. New York: Modern Language Association of America, 1983.

Rossner, Judith (1983). *August.* Boston: Houghton Mifflin.

Ruitenbeek, Hendrik, ed. (1964). *Psychoanalysis and Literature,* New York: Dutton.

Rumelhart, David E. (1977). *Introduction to Human Information Processing.* New York: Wiley.

Rycroft, Charles (1968). *A Critical Dictionary of Psycho-Analysis.* Totowa NJ: Littlefield, Adams.

—— (1974). "Is Freudian Symbolism a Myth?" *New York Review of Books* 24 January: 13-15.

—— (1979). *The Innocence of Dreams.* New York: Pantheon.

Sartre, Jean-Paul (1984). *Le scénario Freud.* Série: La Psychanalyse dans son histoire. Collection dirigée par J.-B. Pontalis. Paris: Gallimard. *The Freud Scenario.* Trans. Quentin Hoare. Chicago: U of Chicago P, 1985.

Schachtel, Ernest G. (1959). *Metamorphosis: On the Development of Affect, Perception, Attention, and Memory.* New York: Basic Books.

Schafer, Roy (1968). "The Mechanisms of Defense." *International Journal of Psycho-Analysis* 49: 49-62.

—— (1970). "An Overview of Heinz Hartmann's Contributions to Psychoanalysis." *International Journal of Psycho-Analysis* 51: 425-446.

—— (1976). *A New Language for Psychoanalysis*. New Haven and London: Yale UP.

—— (1978). *Language and Insight*. The Sigmund Freud Memorial Lectures 1975-1976, University College, London. New Haven and London: Yale UP.

Schank, Roger, and Robert P. Abelson (1977). *Scripts, Plans, Goals, and Understanding: An Inquiry into Human Knowledge Structures*. Hillsdale, NJ: Lawrence Erlbaum.

Schimek, Jean G. (1975). "A Critical Re-Examination of Freud's Concept of Unconscious Mental Representation." *International Review of Psycho-Analysis* 2: 171-187.

Schneiderman, Stuart (1983). *Jacques Lacan: The Death of an Intellectual Hero*. Cambridge, MA: Harvard UP.

Schur, Max (1972). *Freud: Living and Dying*. New York: International UP.

Schwartz, Murray M. (1975). "Where is Literature?" *College English* 36: 756-765.

—— and Coppélia Kahn, eds. (1980). *Representing Shakespeare: New Psychoanalytic Essays*. Baltimore: Johns Hopkins UP.

—— and David Willbern (1982). "Literature and Psychology." *Interrelations of Literature*. J.-P. Barricelli and J. Gibaldi, eds. New York: Modern Language Association of America, pp. 205-224.

Segers, Rien T. (1975). "Readers, Text, and Author: Some Implications of *Rezeptionsästhetik*." *Yearbook of Comparative and General Literature* 24: 15-23.

Sharpe, Ella Freeman (1950). "Psycho-Physical Problems Revealed in Language: An Examination of Metaphor." *Collected Papers on Psycho-Analysis*. London: Hogarth P. 155-169.

Shem, Samuel (1985). *Fine*. New York: St. Martin's/Marek.

Sheridan, Alan (1966). Trans. note: "Imaginary, Symbolic, Real." *Écrits: A Selection*. New York: Norton, 1977. ix-x.

Sievers, W. David (1955). *Freud on Broadway: A History of Psychoanalysis and the American Drama*. New York: Hermitage House.

Silhol, Robert (1984). *Le texte du désir: la critique après Lacan*. Petit Roeulx, Belgium: CISTRE.

Skura, Meredith Anne (1981). *The Literary Use of the Psychoanalytic Process*. New Haven and London: Yale UP.

Smith, Frank (1982). *Understanding Reading: A Psycholinguistic Analysis of Reading and Learning to Read*. 3d ed. New York: Holt, Rinehart, and Winston.

Spector, Jack J. (1973). *The Aesthetics of Freud*. New York: Praeger.

Spiro, Rand J., Bertram C. Bruce, and William F. Brewer, eds. (1980). *Theoretical Issues in Reading Comprehension: Perspectives from Cognitive Psychology, Linguistics, Artificial Intelligence, and Education*. Hillsdale NJ: Lawrence Erlbaum.

Spitz, René A. (1965). *The First Year of Life: A Psychoanalytic Study of Normal and Deviant Development of Object Relations*. New York: International UP.

Steadman, Ralph (1979). *Sigmund Freud*. New York: Simon and Schuster/Touchstone.

Stern, Daniel N. (1971). "A Micro-analysis of Mother-infant Interaction: Behaviors Regulating Social Contact Between a Mother
and her Three-and-a-half-month-old Twins." *Journal of
American Academy of Child Psychiatry* 10: 501-517.

—— (1985). *The Interpersonal World of the Infant: A View from Psychoanalysis and Developmental Psychology*. New York: Basic
Books.

Sternberg, Robert J., ed. (1985). *Human Abilities: An Information-
Processing Approach*. New York: W. H. Freeman.

Strachey, James (1953-1974). Editorial Annotations, "Unconscious." *Standard Edition of the Complete Psychological Works of
Sigmund Freud* 14: 161-165; 12: 258-259; 19: 3-11.

—— (1961). "List of Writings by Freud Dealing Mainly or Largely
with Art, Literature or the Theory of Aesthetics." *Std. Edn.* 21:
213-214.

Suleiman, Susan R., and Inge Crosman, eds. (1980). *The Reader in
the Text: Essays on Audience and Interpretation*. Princeton NJ:
Princeton UP.

Svevo, Italo [Schmitz, Ettore] (1930). *Confessions of Zeno*. New
York: Knopf.

Taylor, Insup, and M. Martin Taylor (1983). *The Psychology of
Reading*. New York: Academic P.

Tennenhouse, Leonard, ed. (1976). *The Practice of Psychoanalytic
Criticism*. Detroit: Wayne State UP.

Thomas, D. M. (1981). *The White Hotel*. New York: Viking P.

Thorburn, M. J. (1925). *Art and the Unconscious: A Psychological Approach to a Problem of Philosophy*. London: Kegan Paul.

Tompkins, Jane P., ed. (1980). *Reader-Response Criticism: From Formalism to Post-Structuralism*. Baltimore: Johns Hopkins UP.

Trilling, Lionel (1953). "Freud and Literature." "Art and Neurosis." *The Liberal Imagination*. New York: Viking P.

Turkle, Sherry (1978). *Psychoanalytic Politics: Freud's French Revolution*. New York: Basic Books.

Waelder, Robert (1930). "Das Prinzip der Mehrfachen Funktion." *Internationale Zeitschrift für Psychanalyse* 16: 286-300. "The Principle of Multiple Function: Observations on Over-Determination." *Psychoanalytic Quarterly* 5 (1936): 45-62.

—— (1960, 1964). *Basic Theory of Psychoanalysis*. New York: International UP; Schocken Books, 1964.

—— (1965). *Psychoanalytic Avenues to Art*. New York: International UP.

Weill, Kurt (1941). *Lady in the Dark*. Musical play by Moss Hart. Lyrics by Ira Gershwin. Vocal score (edited by Albert Sirmay). New York, Chappell & Co., Inc.

White, Hayden V. (1978). *Tropics of Discourse: Essays in Cultural Criticism*. Baltimore: Johns Hopkins UP.

—— (1987). *The Content of the Form: Narrative Discourse and Historical Representation*. Baltimore: Johns Hopkins UP.

Wilson, Edmund (1929). *The Wound and the Bow*. New York: Oxford UP.

—— (1948). "Morose Ben Jonson." *The Triple Thinkers*. New York: Scribner's.

Winner, Ellen (1982). *Invented Worlds: The Psychology of the Arts*. Cambridge MA: Harvard UP.

Winnicott, Donald W. (1953). "Transitional Objects and Transitional Phenomena." *International Journal of Psycho-Analysis* 34: 89-97. Rev. *Playing and Reality*. London: Tavistock, 1971. Ch. 1, 1-25.

—— (1966). "The Location of Cultural Experience." *International Journal of Psycho-Analysis* 48 (1967): 368-372. Rev. *Playing and Reality*. London: Tavistock, 1971. Ch. 7, 95-103.

—— (1980). *Playing and Reality*. London and New York: Tavistock Publications.

Winson, Jonathan (1985). *Brain and Psyche: The Biology of the Unconscious*. Garden City NY: Anchor P/Doubleday.

Wolfenstein, Martha, and Nathan Leites (1950). *Movies: A Psychological Study*. Glencoe IL: Free P.

Wolff, Cynthia Griffin (1977). *A Feast of Words: The Triumph of Edith Wharton*. New York: Oxford UP.

—— (1986). *Emily Dickinson*. New York: Knopf.

Wolff, Peter H. (1960). *The Developmental Psychologies of Jean Piaget and Psychoanalysis*. *Psychological Issues* 2, no. 1. Monograph 5.

Wollheim, Richard (1971). *Sigmund Freud*. Modern Masters Series, ed. Frank Kermode. New York: Viking P.

—— (1979). "The Cabinet of Dr. Lacan." *New York Review of Books* January 25: 36-45.

Wright, Elizabeth E. (1984). *Psychoanalytic Criticism: Theory in Practice*. London and New York: Methuen.